*Quality Education
for All Americans*

Quality Education
for
All Americans

*An Assessment of Gains of Black Americans
with Proposals for Program Development in
American Schools and Colleges for the Next
Quarter-Century*

William F. Brazziel

WASHINGTON, D.C.
Howard University Press
1974

LIBRARY OF CONGRESS CATALOGING IN PUBLICATION DATA

Brazziel, William F.
  Quality education for all Americans.

  Includes bibliographical references.
  1. Negroes—Education. I. Title.
LC2801.B77   370′.973   73-88966
ISBN 0-88258-007-8

Grateful acknowledgment is made to the following for permission to reprint material:

Bureau of Labor Statistics: Charts and graphs from *Black Americans: A Decade of Occupational Change,* U.S. Department of Labor, 1972.

Council of Basic Education: Extract from "Inner-City Children Can Be Taught To Read: Four Successful Schools" by George Weber.

Long Group Limited: Figures from *From Birth to Seven* by Ronald Davie, Neville Butler and Harvey Goldstein.

Jane Mercer: Extract from "Socio-Cultural Factors in Testing Black and Chicano Children," a paper published by the National Education Association for their Tenth Annual Convention, February 18, 1972, Washington, D.C.

National Leadership Institute/Teacher Education: Graphs by Merles B. Karnes. Reprinted by permission of the National Leadership Institute/Teacher Education, University of Connecticut.

The Plain Truth: Excerpts from "Learn, Baby, Learn" by Clifford C. Marcussen and John Kilburn.

From DISTAR™ READING I, Teacher's Guide by Siegfried Engelmann and Elaine C. Bruner. © 1969, Science Research Associates, Inc. Reprinted by permission of the publisher.

From DISTAR™ LANGUAGE I, Teacher's Guide by Siegfried Engelmann and Elaine C. Bruner. © 1972, 1969, Science Research Associates, Inc. Reprinted by permission of the publisher.

Preface

D RAMATIC improvement in the education of black Americans is one of the success stories of the past decade. This improvement is a tribute to the hard work, imaginative planning, and social concerns of many people. The future looks promising for further progress in quality education for black Americans.

Importantly, educators and the community at large must maintain the effort, dedication, and level of resources built up over the years. Black children and youths depend heavily on these infusions of resources and their resulting programs to get a good education. Involved citizens must also step off in new directions to assure quality education to the one-third of the black community that is mired in poverty. A combination of economic and educational programs will assure rapid progress of this segment toward better schooling and a better life.

This book was written for concerned individuals who are interested in making the last quarter-century a time of sustained drives toward true quality education for every black child, youth, and adult. The book examines the sources of schooling such as networks of metropolitan colleges and cradle schools. The reciprocal relationship of education and economic well-being is examined. Roles and responsibilities for business, government, schools, and the black community itself are suggested. Strongly urged is a rapid adoption of the more accurate methods of testing minority students and more insightful methods of evaluating the work of the schools.

Throughout the book, the excellent progress that has been made in the last decade or so is documented and held up as a foundation from which to launch future programs and spur further progress. The dramatic increases in average years of schooling of blacks, similar increases in college enrollment, and the increases in programs of continuing and alternative education give heart to planners and supporters of the quality-education drive.

v

Of course, many needs remain. Indeed, concern for the quality of education for black children and youth must be as constant through the years as concern for the quality of education for white children and youth. Work-force demands and societal shifts, now occurring at an ever swifter pace, require shifts in the emphasis, forms, and patterns of schooling. The concern for excellence is always apparent.

Gifted black children are not being identified and afforded the proper programs and support. Staffing practices and other administrative failures sometimes render school integration counterproductive. Schooling for blacks—like schooling for whites—proceeds best in families that are comfortable economically. This situation in turn depends on equality of opportunity for blacks in the marketplace. The testing programs in many schools are counterproductive for both black and white children. Some school personnel seem inclined to rule rather than serve the people. Both school personnel and the media tend more and more to dwell on the failures instead of the successes in the school enterprise.

Societal shifts demand that concerned citizens also step off in new directions. Most blacks now live in metropolitan areas, but many of the colleges that might serve them well are still in rural areas and small towns. New metropolitan colleges are needed. Blacks and whites must more and more depend on continuing education for the lifelong learning necessary for resuming education interrupted by various intrusions and for updating skills in a rapidly changing marketplace. New forms of evaluation of the school enterprise are demanded. New business-school-government partnerships must be forged to focus on the reciprocal relationships of economics and quality education. Some excellent school programs for poor children of all races are hampered by natterings of social scientists determined to use these programs to prove or disprove some theory entirely unrelated to the thrust of the enterprise. Community social energies must be galvanized and properly utilized. Leadership in both black and white communities is vitally important. Societal thrusts of this magnitude require careful planning. Every possible situation must be anticipated. Improvisation in the face of unforeseen difficulties must be encouraged and perhaps rehearsed.

The author hopes that people who work with a variety of civic concerns and projects will find much of what is said here interesting and valuable because these groups create the climate for strides forward in education. The author hopes that government and corporate planners will find the book helpful along with the captains of these institutions. A special chapter is devoted to an agenda for a schools-government-industry partnership. A heavy emphasis is placed on tying progress in schooling to progress in the economic arena. The author hopes, of course, that every teacher and administrator with responsibility for the education of black children and youth will read the book. The last five years have seen remarkable strides in the development of effective programs from the cradle to graduate education. Important laws have been passed regarding quality in methods of measuring children's capabilities. The author has attempted to identify and record the best of all this. The author hopes, finally, that people who train teachers and administrators will read *Quality Education for All Americans*. The attitudes of many teachers and administrators work to the detriment of black children and youth. These attitudes were often learned at the feet of teacher trainers. In other cases, they are able to find access to schools because of dereliction in the screening of prospective teachers in colleges and universities. Teacher trainers also shape the panoply of skills and techniques teachers carry into the classrooms. Hopefully, the techniques of the excellent programs described in the following chapters on quality school programs, continuing education, and evaluation will become a part of teacher repertoires through preservice training for prospective teachers and in-service training for those already in the classroom.

Hopefully, this book will give hope and spur effective planning for the last quarter-century. Bringing about quality education for black Americans is quite possible during these years. Americans everywhere might warm to this task as never before.

Books that analyze volumes of data and set forth programs

for the future are rarely the products of a single mind. *Quality Education for All Americans* is no different in this respect. Many creative minds contributed to its development. Roberta Palm, Howard University Press editor, and Carole Renca, research assistant at the National Leadership Institute in Teacher Education (NLITE), spent the better part of a year thinking about what should go into (or come out of) the book and how best these things could be said.

Francia Hunter and Rose Goldsher, also of NLITE, combined with Renca to compile the huge amounts of data from which material for the book was selected. This work was especially valuable in the effort to comb the country for the most effective ongoing programs for black children and youth. No stone was left unturned in this research.

Quality Education for All Americans should eventually enable more black children and youth to get topnotch educations. They will owe a debt of gratitude to Charles F. Harris, director of Howard University Press, for his foresight in deciding to direct the resources of the Press to the publication of the book. Yet another shrill litany on the need for reforms has sales value and is a temptation to a publisher. But solid analysis and sound plans for the future will help the black community more at this point in time.

W. F. B.

Contents

xii   *Contents*

Problems of the Competitive Spirit
Annual Education-Economic Audits

Figures

Quality Education
for All Americans

CHAPTER 1

Three Quarter-Century Imperatives

AMERICANS from Africa and large numbers of European-Americans are locked in an earnest struggle to overcome nearly four centuries of neglect and exploitation of the black 12 percent of the American population. This work began in earnest in the early 1960s and has steadily gathered force and strength. The purpose of this book is to assess the situation along the education front, to identify and analyze successes in this area, and to consider possible strategies for the last quarter of the century. The efforts of the last decade have produced some heartening results. Black high-school graduation rates have soared from 36 to 62 percent.[1] College enrollment has nearly doubled, and educators in many schools seem to have solved the riddle of ameliorating the mangling effects of poverty on the aptitude and achievements of children and youth. For the first time in history, there are more black professional, technical, crafts, and operative workers than semiskilled and unskilled workers.

Many hard problems remain, however. More young people must finish their high-school work. More must go on to college and more must function at higher levels of cognitive development. Economic and social development depends upon a highly educated black work force.

Quite possibly the job will be more difficult in years to come. Many of the shining successes of midcentury were achieved by black middle-class families and their children and by poverty-

1

ridden but strongly upward-mobile families that somehow sum-
moned the strength and fortitude to boost their children into the
middle class. Success in the future will likely depend on a close
linkage of economic and educational programs.

Demythologizing the Schools

The first step in gaining proper perspective on the job to be
done is to slough off the historical myths and legends surrounding city schools and poor people. To understand how myths and
legends can warp perspective and hamper planning, one might
read carefully *The Great School Legend* by Colin Greer.[2] Greer
is director of the University Without Walls of the City University of New York.

Contrary to popular and carefully nurtured beliefs, American
schools did not receive millions of poor immigrants from England, Europe, and American farms and transform them into
the productive middle class of generations later, Greer contends.
School records show that schools, with a few exceptions, failed
miserably in attempts to offer quality education to the children
of these poor families. The records included cumulative folders,
analyses of standardized testing, IQ scores, in-grade retention,
and children labeled retarded—accurately and otherwise. Economic opportunities, unions, and in some cases grants of free
land created the middle class where it exists today for the
descendants of the newcomers to the city.

Greer presents data on some ten national ethnic groups in
America ranging alphabetically from English to Welsh. The
struggle for an education for the children of these ethnic groups
in city schools is instructive to those working to deliver quality
education in cities today.

Failure rates, test scores, and graduation rates left much to
be desired in these schools. The number of "normal" children
in 1890, for example, ranged from a high of only 60 percent in
the Chicago schools to a low of 35 percent in Minneapolis. One
1943 survey showed 90 percent of the New York children

below national norms on tests. A 1912 survey showed the graduation rates ranging from less than 1 percent for one ethnic group to a grand high of 15 percent for the most bookish group. By comparison, today's schools are far more successful and far more humanized.

Historically, most of the school successes of the new American dwellers came in the second generation and only after solid economic gains had been made by parents of the children involved. Where these gains were not forthcoming, Greer notes, school performance of immigrant and rural in-migrant descendants leaves much room for improvement today.

Greer notes that economic advancement of the newcomers depended heavily on the skills they brought with them and on the demand for these skills in the American economy. A confluence of skills and demands meant rapid advancement, as in the case of Germans who came to America from urban centers bringing entrepreneurial skills, capital in some cases, and a ready-made adjustment to urban life. Immigrants from rural areas had a more difficult time. One exception was the Scandinavian immigrant to the upper Midwest who benefitted from the rich land grants of the 1850s and was able to put his farming talents to work and develop productive holdings in a short time. English, Scottish, and Welsh families who settled in Appalachian farms and mines had the reverse experience.

Studies of this sort indicate the lesson of history is to appraise realistically and promote the role of economics in the development of black and other minorities and to urge planners to develop stratagems for promoting simultaneous economic and educational development for these families and their children. Together these stratagems become synergistic, as evidenced by some current success stories. Greer notes it is very difficult to deliver quality education to poor children and it is equally as difficult to avoid delivering quality education to those in more fortunate circumstances. By historical standards, programs for poor children are far more effective today than anything that has ever happened in American schools, but a clear concept of what really happened and of the entwinement of economics and education is crucial for a proper perspective in current efforts.

Encouraging Trends

Between 1960 and 1970, black workers made encouraging gains in higher-paid and middle-level occupations. Black professional, technical, and managerial workers increased 109 percent, and clerical, sales, craftsmen, and operative personnel increased 64 percent. White workers showed 31 and 21 percent gains respectively for this period (see Figures 1 and 2). Also in this decade, black laborers and domestic workers showed a 15 percent decrease. The number of white workers in this low-paid category showed a 3 percent rise (see Figures 1 and 2).

In 1970, improved education and better occupational distribution of black workers lessened the impact of unemployment, according to U.S. Labor Department statistics. The rate pegged at 8.2 percent is estimated to have been 10 percent if the levels of education and the severity of job discrimination had been the same as in 1960 (see Figure 3).

The 62 percent graduation rate for black youth has narrowed the education gap for young adults to less than one-half year. Blacks in the twenty-five-to-twenty-nine-year-old category averaged 12.1 years of schooling; whites averaged 12.4. Valuable schooling is also being received by blacks in the military, the Job Corps, and manpower training programs, all of which enroll large numbers of black youth and young adults (see Figure 3).

Black college enrollment increased from 232,000 to over 500,000 between 1964 and 1972, and in spite of booming white enrollments during this period, black proportions of college students rose from 5 to 7 percent of total enrollment.[3]

Labor Department statisticians estimate that 75 percent of young black adults will have four or more years of high school by 1980 with corresponding increases in earning power (see Figure 4).

Encouragingly too, a larger percent of the black force in 1980 will consist of younger and better-educated blacks. While

FIGURE 1
BLACK OCCUPATIONAL GAINS, 1960–1970

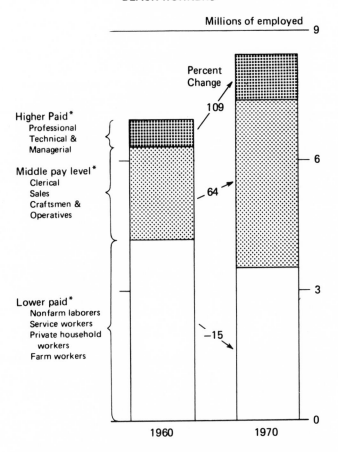

BLACK WORKERS

. . . while the number of black workers in lower-paid occupations decreased.

SOURCE: *Black Americans: A Decade of Occupational Change,* U.S. Department of Labor, 1972.

FIGURE 2
WHITE OCCUPATIONAL GAINS, 1960–1970

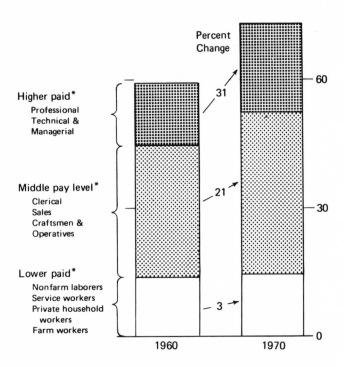

WHITE WORKERS

Millions of employed

... but the share and number of white workers employed in the higher-paid occupations continued to be much larger than for black workers.

SOURCE: *Black Americans: A Decade of Occupational Change,* U.S. Department of Labor, 1972.

FIGURE 3
BLACK EDUCATIONAL GAINS, 1940–1970

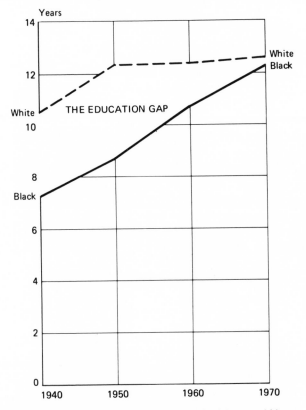

**MEDIAN YEARS OF SCHOOL COMPLETED BY YOUNG ADULTS
(25–29 YEARS OLD)**

By 1970, educational attainment of young black adults was within one-half of young white people this age. Lack of education is often a barrier to employment in better paid jobs for both black and white workers, whether education is required for performance of the job or not.

SOURCE: *Black Americans: A Decade of Occupational Change*, U.S. Department of Labor, 1972.

FIGURE 4
PROJECTED BLACK EDUCATIONAL GAINS, 1970–1980

PERCENT HAVING 4 YEARS OF HIGH SCHOOL OR MORE, AGES 25-34

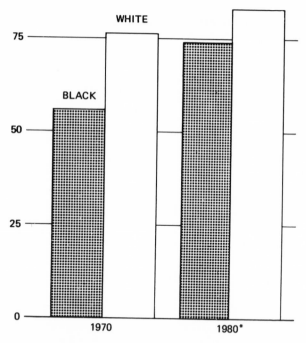

As a result, a larger proportion of black workers is expected to be in the better paid occupations.

*Projection

SOURCE: *Black Americans: A Decade of Occupational Change,* U.S. Department of Labor, 1972.

45 percent of the black work force consisted of these workers in 1960, they will comprise nearly 60 percent of the workers in 1980.[4]

Work Yet to Be Done

The challenge to the black community and whites of good will is to build upon the momentum of the 1960s and drive toward realizable goals of comparability in education, income, and general social well-being. Comparisons of black-white status in these areas will reveal gaps that need to be filled in some instances. In other cases full comparability in an area might not be completely desirable because the situation as it exists may not be serving whites well. College attendance is a case in point. Authorities lament that too many whites are being forced into college attendance because of social and parental pressures. The "reluctant student" has become a byword in academic circles. Four million teachers will be produced by colleges in the next ten years for two million vacancies, for example.

A less simplistic method of setting goals would be to analyze labor-force projections and prepare black youth to compete to the fullest in heavy-demand occupations with good salaries. Credentialing goals may take a different direction also. A less futile and surely a less frustrating effort to assure high-school credentials for a larger number of black youth may be to turn from increased money and programs for public schools and concentrate on programs for students who leave school for work and other pursuits. Some efforts toward this consideration apparently are already in motion. Over 230,000 high-school equivalency diplomas were awarded last year, about one-third of which went to black youth and young adults. The education system seems to be graduating nearly half as many blacks in General Education Development (GED) programs as are coming out of American high schools. Conscious planning for this pluralistic form of credentialing should yield even greater results.

Insightful analyses of this sort may yield good results in the development of goals in the jobs category. Gross discrimination is lessening for blacks seeking entry-level jobs in government and large corporations. Smaller firms use a variety of stratagems to discriminate, however. Both large and small firms in the South practice discrimination. Further, promotion and access to training programs leading to promotion will need attention. A success story of the 1960s was constituted by the 550,000 or so young adult families who were matching their white counterparts in earnings as of the 1970 census. All of these young people were under thirty-five years of age. Meaningful programs would assure that promotion and salary increases through the years enable the census to find the same or higher figures for these families in 1980 when they are in the forty-five-year-old category and in 1990 when they should be in their peak earning years.

Education Goals

Analysts predict that more than 90 percent of the young adult white workers will have four or more years of schooling by the year 2000. The American work force will also have about 25 percent of its members holding college degrees and 10 percent with at least a master's degree. Ph.D. production is in such a state of flux at present that it is difficult to make predictions for the next twenty-eight years. Obviously, the percentage of Ph.D.'s—employed and otherwise—will be higher than the one-half of one per cent now present in the work force.

Four or more years of schooling for 90 percent of young black adults might be realistic and beneficial. As stated previously, graduation rates for black youth are 62 percent, and at present rates of increases black workers will approach the 80 percent mark by 1980. The challenge to planners and school administrators is to insure the 1980 figure plus an additional 10 percent. A linear plan for these increases might look as follows:

Percentage of American Work Force (Ages 24–29)
with Four or More Years of School

Year	Percentage
1972	62
1982	82
1992	87
2002	90

The plan tapers off after 1982 and aims at a 5 percent and then 3 percent increase per decade to allow for the increases in severity of problems as more and more of the very poor black youth attempt to secure a high-school diploma through the regular high school or one of the continuation programs.

Goals for Black Workers

Educational forecasters might possibly estimate the dimensions of the education and training efforts needed to enable black workers and entrepreneurs to build on the gains of mid-century. The job is challenging but quite manageable, and comparability in some areas is possible by the year 2000.

The American work force is expected to hit 95 million by mid-1980, and if current low trends in birth rates are an indication, growth during the last fifteen years should be quite gradual. Approximately 15 million professional and technical workers, 27 million clerical and sales, 12 million craftsmen and foremen, and 9 million managers and proprietors will be a part of the work force. Service jobs such as policemen, firemen, and hospital attendants will involve the energies of another 11 million.

Proportional black participation in these jobs requires increases in the pace related to equal access to employment, increases in promotion of blacks to clear the portals for new entries, and substantial increases in programs and policies to spur black entrepreneurism in business enterprises.

Comparability in black labor-force participation may be a

realistic goal by the year 2000. This estimate assumes a slow increase in labor-force growth after 1980.

To achieve this goal, blacks would need to add 1.09 million professional and technical workers to the 766,000 now operating in the labor force. This figure works out to approximately 360,000 additions each decade and compares favorably to the 416,000 new black workers added to this cadre between 1960 and 1970. A figure of 390,000 would allow for a retirement rate of 6,000 workers per year. This rather low number reflects the relative youth of the new cadres in this area (see Figure 5).

FIGURE 5
GOALS FOR BLACK WORKERS

Occupational Category	Number Employed			Needed Increase
	1960	1970	Goals for 2000 *	
Professional and Technical	360,000	766,000	1,856,000	1,090,000
Managers and Proprietors	182,000	298,000	1,140,000	842,000
Clerical and Sales	700,000	1,292,000	2,076,000	784,000
Craftsmen and Foremen	420,000	691,000	1,464,000	773,000
Service Workers (police, fire, hotel, etc.)	1,200,000	1,547,000	1,332,000	215,000
Operatives (machines, truck drivers, etc.)	1,998,000	2,004,000	1,848,000	−156,000

SOURCE: Data from *Social and Economic Status of Negroes in the United States,* U.S. Department of Labor, 1971.

* Computations based on 12 percent black proportion of a projected minimum work force of 95 million by categories; e.g., 1,856,000 black professional and technical workers represent about 12 percent of 15.5 million projected for work force.

A net total of 842,000 managers and proprietors, 784,000 clerical and sales workers, 773,000 craftsmen and foremen, and 215,000 service workers must be added. A net decrease of 156,000 in the operatives category is indicated. Increases of

300,000 managers and proprietors per decade and approximately 250,000 each for clerical and sales and craftsmen and foremen are indicated. Only 72,500 additional service workers per decade will be needed. Comparable increases were made in all of these categories from 1960 to 1970, with the exception of managers and proprietors where less than one-third (108,000) of this indicated increase was made (see Figure 6).

FIGURE 6
INCREASES AND PROJECTED INCREASES OF BLACK WORKERS

Occupational Category	Needed Increase for Comparability	Number Each Decade	Increase Last Decade (1960–1970)
Professional and Technical	1,094,000	360,000	416,000
Managers and Proprietors	842,000	300,000	108,000
Clerical and Sales	784,000	250,000	592,000
Craftsmen and Foremen	773,000	250,000	271,000
Service Workers	215,000	72,000	347,000
Operatives	None	None	16,000

SOURCE: Data from *Social and Economic Status of Negroes in the United States,* U.S. Department of Labor, 1971.

Education and Training Prospects

Can American schools and colleges produce 1,090,000 black professional and technical workers in the next thirty years? It would seem reasonable to say yes to this question, especially if additional resources are expended, as suggested in Chapter 4.

This view assumes that American corporations will continue their efforts in equal opportunity, that federal, state, and local governments do the same, and that black entrepreneurism is increased to provide for more jobs in black-directed business enterprises and for more self-employed black professionals.

Notably, the prospects for comparability in the medical and

legal professions are not quite as bright, although considerable progress can be made. Law and medical school enrollments must be increased dramatically in a time of a shortage of class places to train the students.

Who will educate the new workers in this category? American colleges, black and white, and a new network of metropolitan colleges described in Chapter 4 will do the job. Approximately 35,000 black college graduates annually will be required and black colleges alone produce 20,000 at present. Strangely, no one really knows the annual black baccalaureate production of white colleges. Further, the enrollment situation is in a state of transition. As of 1970, however, U.S. Office of Education analysts commonly stated that black colleges produced 70 percent of the total number of new black baccalaureates. Total production using this yardstick, then, would have been about 28,500.

Prospects for training clerical and sales workers and craftsmen and foremen seem manageable, although the latter categories depend heavily on equal opportunity in union-controlled apprenticeship programs and in promotion practices in various industries. Clerical and sales workers are trained by high schools, proprietary schools, technical institutes, manpower programs, and a variety of para-school programs, as well as by business and industry itself. A net addition of 784,000 will not present a problem if all sectors of the educational and commercial worlds cooperate. The addition of 300 black clerical workers by each of the 2,500 largest corporations could absorb these workers. The 80,000 government units in America, the 19,000 or so school systems, the armed services, and the federal government also need this sort of manpower.

The same case can be made for service workers, and as noted above, the number of operatives should actually decrease. Also missing in analyses to this point has been the mention of farm and mine workers and unskilled laborers. The proportion of blacks in these jobs is dropping sharply and will continue in this vein.

The big challenge in this drive is going to be the net addition of 842,000 managers and proprietors. While the business schools and colleges can do yeoman's service here, entrepreneurism requires a fortunate combination of know-how, demand, capital, and business contacts. Every other business that sets up shop in America finally folds its tent. According to *World Book Encyclopedia,* the 500,000 people going into business each year pass (in the night one presumes) an equal number on their way out of the business sector.[5] Many more blacks must get onto this wavelength. The Small Business Administration (SBA) is working hard in this area. The corporations and government agencies must also promote more blacks to managerial positions.

The latter groups can also serve mightily in availing future black businessmen of both training and badly needed business contacts. More and more of the new black entrepreneurs are graduates of corporate structures, antipoverty programs, and city and federal governments. The future pattern may well be college, five years at General Motors, and a spin-off with SBA help into a self-owned consulting or marketing firm.

The new metropolitan colleges discussed later could perform yeoman's service with their business schools and new urban extension services designed to deal with the myriad peculiarities of black business in white America.

Focal Points for the Last Quarter-Century

Strategies are important in planning of such magnitude. Care in the selection of goals is demanded. Mistakes must be kept to a minimum and improvisation when things go awry must be skillful. The game plan is not so unlike the black American strategies in the last quarter-century. Synergism is the order of the day. Success must breed success. Successful strategies must be replicated again and again. Forces must be deployed at key points to trigger watersheds in certain areas. Meaningless controversies must be avoided.

Many of these strategies are discussed in detail in Chapter 7. Some strategies involve both blacks and whites, and one is well advised to examine needed pressure points here.

Affirmative-action programs in employment must be intensified at all levels and special attention must be given to the South. Nothing is more important in the education-economic dynamic. Important gains have been made, but many corporations, government agencies, school systems, and private firms use a variety of stratagems to deny blacks employment. Stepped-up activity by the government to enforce equal-employment provisions of the Civil Rights Acts will be of great value. Soon, hopefully, a watershed of sorts will be released with 65 percent of black young adults moving into good jobs and serving as living examples for children and youth in the schools. This move is especially necessary in the South where 52 percent of the black children reside but where less than 40 percent of the young adults have graduated from high school. This figure compares to a high among blacks of 75 percent in Western states. Both figures reflect migration of Southern high-school graduates to Western states, but they mostly reflect the lack of opportunity for blacks to put a diploma to work in the South and the corresponding lack of the most important magnet to young people to finish school. The South is one of the fastest industrializing areas in the country. Blacks simply *must* share in this new growth and prosperity.

Closely related to this dynamic is the need for blacks to emphasize more the development of gifted black children and youth. Gifted youngsters might well be thought of as the top 20 percent of the quick, highly verbal children of each annual crop of black births plus another 5 percent with special abilities of one sort or another. The word *gifted* refers to any person who is superior in some ability that can make him an outstanding contributor to society. This definition broadens the gifted population to include individuals with outstanding abilities in corporate management, politics, the performing arts, and community leadership. Consequently 125,000 of the 500,000 black babies born each year should receive special attention, and fully 1.5 million of the 6 million black children in public schools would be given special attention. A variety of methods may be used to identify these 125,000 youngsters including: teachers' observation of the child's classroom performance, tests measuring creativity administered by school administrators and psychometrists, unusual performance on I.Q. tests, and unusual leadership and creative performance manifested in activities in the community. From this group the additional physicians, lawyers, economists, entrepreneurs, civic leaders, generals, scientists, and other key individuals will come. These children are not being identified and developed. Production of black trained minds in these areas will continue to lag until some action is begun. This problem is discussed in detail in Chapter 2. The South notably poses a dilemma and so does the lack of money.

The Importance of Money

Black students do not enroll in college in great numbers because they don't have the money to do so and because free or inexpensive colleges are not located in their cities. College requires a considerable amount of money and black families don't have the money to spend.

Figure 7 indicates the sad situation in this area. Nearly 87 percent of all youth in families with incomes over $15,000 go

FIGURE 7
WHO GOES TO COLLEGE—EFFECT OF FAMILY INCOME

Percentage of High-School Seniors Entering College by Brackets of Annual Family Income

$15,000 and over	86.7%
$10,000–$15,000	61.3%
$ 7,500–$10,000	51.0%
$ 3,000–$ 7,500	37.7%
Less than $3,000	19.8%

SOURCE: U.S. Census Bureau (Special Report Prepared for U.S. Department of Health, Education, and Welfare).

to college—whether they want to or not. This figure is nearly six times as many as attend in the $3,000-per-year bracket. More ominous for blacks, 61 percent of the students in $10,000–$15,000-income families go to college, but only 37 percent of the students in the $3,000–$7,500-income families go. In 1971, the family incomes of whites rose to $10,200, while black incomes stayed steady at approximately $6,500. In other words, the blacks lost ground in income to generate college applicants and they are making improvements—but still losing ground—in overall production of college graduates.

The Southern Dilemma

In spite of early school leaving and migration of blacks who do graduate, the South is still a heavy producer of black talent. Black colleges, most of which are located in Southern states, produced in the early 1970s 83 percent of the black physicians, 75 percent of eventual black Ph.D. recipients, 75 percent of the black army officers, 65 percent of all black state representatives or senators, one-half of the black Congressional representatives, the only black senator, and 65 percent of all high-ranking federal officials (GS 14 and up, plus Cabinet appointees).

Further, Andrew Billingsley in his *Black Families in White America* has identified forceful and sometimes rigid support of the black Southern church, black teachers, physicians, undertakers, and merchants as powerful generators of achievement in Southern communities and weak or virtually absent factors in many black impacted areas outside the South.[6] Billingsley also found a strong influence on black achievers exerted by black colleges. Large numbers of these individuals came from communities surrounding these colleges. True equal opportunity in the South plus the preservation of black colleges, black businesses, black teachers, and black churches could make the South a showcase of black talent development. At the very least, the critical factors in this dynamic can be recognized and intelligently employed in the drive to bring about larger numbers of well-trained blacks.[7]

New Tests Needed

Individuals interested in greater educational attainment must continue their drives for better methods of measuring black aptitudes and achievements. Since 1950 various testing programs have grown to mammoth proportions for the sorting, grading, and distribution of 1.5 million American freshmen into 2,600 colleges and universities. People over the age of forty will find the magnitude and dangers of this apparatus hard to appreciate. The Educational Testing Service, for example, tested more than one-third of all high-school seniors last year (1.8 million) and grossed $28.5 million in sales. Since 1958, the National Defense Education Act has supplied large sums (about $7 million annually) to school systems to test and sort children. Funds for special-education classes have also been made available.

Blacks have been malsorted (improperly placed) under these new programs. Figures on a national level show that black children for the most part are not assessed accurately by these instruments. Middle-class black children are important exceptions, but presently they constitute less than one-half of the total number tested. As a consequence, large numbers of black students who ordinarily would have entered four-year colleges are forced to settle for a community college—or no college. More ominous is the inordinate number of black children placed in classes for the mentally retarded because of tests. Figures are inexact on the number of black children in these classes. For California, however, the rate of assignment was four times that of whites. California is unusual, to be sure, but it is entirely possible that a large percentage of the black primary children are receiving their education—or noneducation—in these classes and that more than one-half of these children were erroneously placed through maltesting. These children must be rescued. More on this pressure point is included in Chapter 2.

High-Impact Programs for Problem Schools

A final pressure point that may be mentioned at this time is the need to insist that high-impact programs be utilized in problem schools. High-impact programs are intensified instructional programs that increase the volume of practice and learning experiences, involve parents more directly, and bolster school programs with added services such as tutors and specialists for learning disabilities. Again, middle-class black children will need only a standard program and money need not be squandered here. But the deeper into the ghetto one goes, the more acute the need for high-impact education becomes. Many excellent and utterly dependable high-impact programs have been developed in the last decade and they must be used. Many of the ineffective experiments and fads being tested in the schools must be eliminated. For example, one major school system rewarded the children with money in an attempt to raise reading levels.

Notes for Chapter 1

[1] Ben J. Wattenberg and Richard M. Scammon in the article "Black Progress and Liberal Rhetoric" in the April, 1973, issue of *Commentary* magazine note that for the first time in history most blacks can be considered middle class. Their evaluation came from the 1970 census and special surveys completed since then.

[2] Colin Greer, *The Great School Legend* (New York: Basic Books, 1972).

[3] U.S. Department of Labor, *Black Americans: A Decade of Occupational Change,* 1972.

[4] U.S. Department of Labor, *Social and Economic Conditions of Negroes in the United States,* 1971.

[5] *World Book Encyclopedia,* vol. 2 (Chicago: Field Enterprises, 1966), p. 610.

[6] Andrew Billingsley, *Black Families in White America* (Englewood Cliffs, N.J.: Prentice-Hall, Inc., 1968), pp. 103–4.

[7] Ibid.

CHAPTER 2

Quality School Programs

DELIVER is the magic word in coming to grips with the challenge of quality education for black children and youth in the last quarter-century. What programs, what curricula, what school and staff practices will *deliver* in the several types of schools black students will attend in these years? Where are these programs now operating successfully? What are the barriers to successful replication wherever black children are in schools?

To begin, recognition must be given to the fact that all black people and their children are not alike. Albert Murray has sadly noted in his *South to a Very Old Place* that inability to make this distinction is a blind spot and perhaps an Achilles' heel on the part of both black militants and white liberals. Murray notes that too many whites and a few blacks insist on all blacks being treated exactly alike, thereby assuring progress for no one, as most programs are tied to the lowest common denominator.[1] Because of this faulty logic, the daughter of a Long Island engineer can be herded into a program for the "culturally deprived" at her high school or free lunch tickets can be given to all blacks in a similar school. Educators must make these distinctions if effective programs are to be developed.

Diverse programming is as necessary for the many types of black children as it is for the many types of white children. Upper-class black children live in Atlanta, Grosse Pointe, and Scarsdale; upper-middle-class children in the new suburbs, on farms, and in outer reaches of the cities; lower-middle-class children closer in; and some very, very poor children in the center of the city, in migrant camps, and in Southern villages and farming communities.

In all of these social classes and income groups exist the same types of individual differences in interests and aptitudes found elsewhere. Gifted children exist and must be identified and developed. Children lacking in skills highly valued in school must be provided a good educational experience. Parents must be brought into a home-school partnership.

School programming will be simple for middle- and upper-class black children and youth. The usual school program will suffice with perhaps conscious efforts to include more black history and culture in the curriculum and to drive the gifted youngsters harder than previously.

These efforts may seem deceptively simple, however. Most middle- and upper-class black children will probably constitute a minority population in white schools in the years to come because these upper-income black families will be living in the outer city and the suburbs where most whites now live. Multicultural curricula and work with gifted black children will depend heavily on the awareness and mental sets of white teachers and administrators.

Supplementary work by black fraternal and church groups may be needed to insure that integration does not become a counterproductive force for the gifted black child.

The following sections will include an examination of several educational concepts. The author will consider programming needs for black children in standard school programs; make a consideration of integrated education, its values and pitfalls and offer a set of improved practices for integrated education. An analysis is made of effective high-impact programs for very poor black children and youth. Programming for gifted black children from middle and upper classes and from less favored circumstances is also treated as is vocational and special education.

Standard School Programs

Children for which the standard school program is appropriate if modified slightly would fit the following profile:

Family   — One of approximately 535,000 young Northern and Western families matching whites in income; or old establishment families in the South with business, farming, or professional background; or children of strongly upward-mobile factory or service workers

Siblings   — 1.3

Family Income   — $10,000+

Family Aspirations
for Child   — Professions, business, or farm management

Place of Residence — Outer reaches of big city, good residential area of towns, or large farms

About 35 percent of the black families could be classified in this manner in 1970 and the number is growing daily. Between 1960 and 1970, for example, blacks bought nearly 900,000 homes in new subdivisions.[2]

School programs that demand high performance from these children, treat them kindly and humanely, and prepare them for further study will serve the black community well. From this group most of the lawyers, physicians, scientists, generals, politicians, and civic workers must come. Potential exists in all groups and every effort will be made to develop this capacity, but the odds are far better for the production of a surgeon from children in a family of an Atlanta surgeon or businessman than from the children of a welfare family in Watts. However, economic development plus high-impact school programs in Watts will lower these odds.

Middle-class black children must have mental rigor at every point in the school program, and importantly, white and black teachers recognizing the students' talents must demand a lot from these children and confer with their parents if they fail to progress. The importance of differentiating between black children is clear. Differentiation and rigor mean the difference between finally producing enough physicians to care for the black community or struggling along with the present inadequacies.

Two dangers exist that parents, school people, and young blacks themselves must recognize and guard against. First, anger over racial injustices and inordinate expenditures of efforts to correct these injustices may entirely consume some of the most brilliant young people. Adolescence is the dangerous age, and somehow the young prospective surgeon must be made to see that his best contribution to the struggle will be the study and practice of medicine and that time at the barricades, if excessive, *undermines* the drive for equality and justice by wasting another brain on areas that can be manned by lesser talents. Generals, politicians, and leaders of pressure groups are all needed but most are not capable of the academic rigor needed for the professions, and the black community must not waste brains by allowing young people with these talents to consume themselves by either anger or misplaced efforts at leadership.

The second danger rests largely with the performance of the integrated school. As noted previously, most of these high-potential black youngsters will be attending integrated schools. No one has really studied the productivity of these schools where black talent is concerned. Traditionally, black students from middle-class families who attended all-black Armstrong High School in Richmond, Virginia, could be expected to enroll in Virginia State College in large numbers, and a respectable number would finally enroll in the Howard University or Meharry College medical schools. For every three hundred students in an Armstrong class, five might return to Virginia ten years later as practicing physicians. Now that large numbers of able black students attend Thomas Jefferson High School replete with integrated faculty and student body, what is the production rate? What happens in the integrated school, then, assumes great importance.

Integrated Education

Careful longitudinal study of the benefits derived from integrated education by both black and white children will enable planners to execute programs for integrated education more carefully. Sometimes school integration is detrimental to black children. This phenomenon should also be studied carefully.

Potentially, children stand to gain many benefits from integrated schools and the nation can gain even more. Children— black or white—can not be prepared for a dynamic multiracial society by being educated in segregated schools. Donald Morrison, president of the National Education Association, summarizes the counterproductivity of this sort of education as succinctly as any in a guest editorial in *Phi Delta Kappan*. He states the following view:

> School segregation is as wrong educationally as it is constitutionally. It provides a poor learning environment. It instills feelings of inferiority in black chldren and robs them of the confidence they need to learn. It limits their ambitions and aspirations. It gives them a wholly unrealistic concept of the world into which they will emerge upon leaving school. And it has an adverse effect upon the attitudes and expectations of teachers. School segregation also has damaging effects upon white children. It breeds false notions of superiority and unrealistic self-perceptions harmful to their development. It deprives them of the opportunity to learn how to relate to black people, who in adult life will be their coworkers and are increasingly likely to be their supervisors and neighbors. And it induces in white children moral confusion and guilt, which are often reflected in rebellion against parental, educational, and other forms of authority.[3]

Importantly, every effort must be made to develop desegregated schools that have a minimum of racial tension and disharmony. Ideally, each desegregated school would be so organized that each child, black and white, would receive the optimal benefits from school integration. This concept places a responsibility for effective organization on the shoulders of teachers, administrators, school boards, and students. A checklist of responsibilities for each of these groups has been developed by Integrated Education Associates of Chicago. The checklist includes 183 items deemed either essential or highly desirable for integrated schools.[4] Some representative items by areas are listed below:

Principals

1. Show teachers how important they believe integration is for *all* children.
2. Arrange for teacher observation in good integrated schools in other districts.
3. Welcome teachers black and white who may constitute a minority in his school.
4. Constantly explain advantages of integration to teachers and parents.
5. Help teachers develop skills for integrated education through a variety of in-service experiences.

Teachers

1. Recognize that they are important partners in the desegregation process.
2. Are alert to the needs of shy children for whom integrated schools may be stressful.
3. Offer minority teachers (black or white) leadership opportunities.
4. Promptly halt the use of derogatory language about *any* ethnic group.
5. See differences among minority children.
6. Demand equal academic effort for all children.
7. Teach a multicultural curriculum which includes previously excluded material on black contributions to American life.

Superintendents and School Boards

1. Offer opportunities for parents to learn more about the desegregation process.
2. Assign significant numbers of minority administrators, both as principals and in central office positions, including the superintendency.

3. Provide for a special unit to promote human relations in the school system.
4. Speak before a number of groups in the community on the progress and benefits of the desegregated schools.
5. Meet with boards and administrators in good integrated school districts elsewhere.

Students

1. Are given the feeling that they may aspire to every adult role in the school.
2. Regard their teachers as helpful.
3. Offer minority students (black or white) an opportunity for leadership positions.
4. Involve their student councils in problems of school integration.
5. Are able to meet representatives of *all* colleges recruiting students.
6. Involve minority students in all roles in plays and other productions.
7. Have individualized curriculums for gifted minority children.

Curriculum and General School Practices

1. Machinery exists to assess accurately and thoroughly any special needs new children in the school may have.
2. Communications programs spotlight the successes of integrated schools.
3. School staff (clerical and food) are involved in in-service classes on school integration.
4. Dress codes are multicultural.
5. The curriculum is multicultural and multiracial in science and mathematics as well as in social sciences and humanities.

Integrated education can be a wonderful learning experience for black and white children—or a nightmare for both and counterproductive for the nation. Successful school integration depends heavily on the seventeen thousand or so school boards and school superintendents, on their central office lieutenants, and on two million or so American teachers.

Some shining examples of good integrated education do exist, as do disasters in this area. More and more black children will be in integrated schools in the future. Imperatives are indicated for making a sustained effort to assure a good school experience for these children.

Programs for Poor Children

Strangely, the first priority in drives to improve the schooling of large numbers of poor children is the elimination of tests as barriers to the access to the more competent teachers in the schools and to the faster paces and higher expectations in their classrooms. Inaccurate testing relegates inordinate numbers of poor black children to streams, or tracks, or classes for retarded children that insure systematic annual retardation because of low expectations and a slow pace on the part of teachers, many of whom are either substitutes or not fully qualified. Test errors loom big in any plans to improve the schooling of poor black children.

One of the best and most comprehensive studies of errors in testing and labeling minorities was described by Jane Mercer at the National Education Association's Tenth Annual Conference on Human Rights.[5] Mercer has completed a series of three interwoven studies in this area under grants from the National Institute of Mental Health. Her findings are sad but instructive, and they offer guidance to those who need solid data on which to develop accurate psychometric programs for minorities. Schools simply cannot continue to make these mistakes with children. The stakes are too high and the damage is too severe.

Mercer studied all of the minorities labeled mentally retarded by the schools in a city of 100,000 people in California. Two hundred forty-one different organizations serving retarded people in one way or another were then queried regarding their clientele. Of the 429 persons labeled retarded by the schools, 340 had not been so labeled by any other agency in the city.

Mercer and her associates then developed an adaptive behavior measure to see if minorities labeled retarded in the schools were performing normally after they left the schools. *Adaptive behavior* was defined here as the ability to play ever more complex roles in a progressively widening circle of social systems. The instruments included twenty eight age-graded scales.

Sixty percent of the Chicanos and 91 percent of the blacks labeled retarded by the schools passed the adaptive behavior measures, while *none* of the Anglos passed the measures. These scales were used to survey a representative sample of 6,907 persons from the community and involved insightful comparisons of black, white, and Chicano adults labeled retarded by the schools during their attendance at these institutions.

Eighty percent of the first two groups had been graduated from high school and had a job. Sixty-five percent were white-collar workers. All were able to work without supervision, participate in sports, travel alone, and shop intelligently. All visited with coworkers, friends, and neighbors. In other words, their social-role performance was indistinguishable from other adults in the community *in spite* of the fact that the schools had erroneously labeled them retarded. Mercer concluded that IQ testing for assignment to classes for the mentally retarded was accurate for Anglos but highly inaccurate for minorities.

Mercer's team then analyzed general minority performance on IQ tests after grouping a six thousand black and Chicano sample on five modal characteristics indicating similarity of family life-styles to those of the dominant Anglo-Saxon population. Children from families with only one life-style characteristic averaged 82.7 on the tests, those from families with three averaged 92.8, while children from families with all five characteristics had a mean of 99.5, the same as the Anglo population. Mercer concludes that rather than a measure of abilities, IQ tests, for most minorities, are a measure of the degree of "Anglocized" life-styles (see Figure 8).

FIGURE 8
CONVERGENCE OF THE AVERAGE IQ TEST SCORES OF BLACK CHILDREN WITH THE STANDARD NORMS AS SOCIOCULTURAL FACTORS ARE INCREASINGLY CONTROLLED

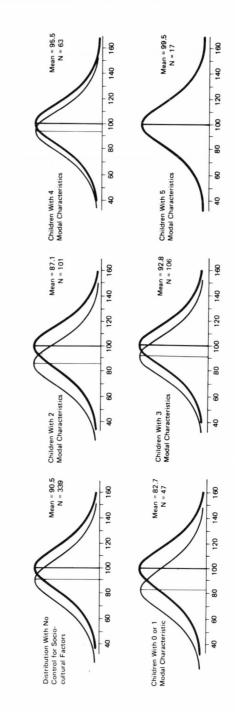

SOURCE: Jane Mercer, "Socio-Cultural Factors in Testing Black and Chicano Children," paper published by the National Education Association for their Tenth Annual Convention, February 18, 1972, Washington, D.C.

More on avoiding mistakes of the sort evidenced in Mercer's report is included in Chapter 5. Clearly, however, quality education for poor children will often simply be unavailable because of unfortunate school practices. As noted in the subsequent chapter, the first step a wise administrator will take in assuming command in a school with poor children is to substitute readiness tests for IQ tests and criterion-referenced tests for achievement tests.

The second step is to apply a high-impact program designed to move the children along at a rapid rate and to fill in the gaps in their development that is the legacy of poverty.

High-Impact Programs

High-impact programs are being developed at an increasingly rapid rate as researchers and developers find the range in their drives to develop curricula that will enable poor children to succeed in school. A casual profile of a poor child most in need of such a program might look as follows:

Family   — One of the 1.2 million black families mired
                in poverty
Siblings   — 4.1
Birth Order — Fourth child
Sex   — Male
Place of
Residence   —Downtown apartment in large city or tenant
                shack on a Southern farm

This child is likely to be exceeded in reading by his more fortunate counterpart in the black middle class by as much as three full years by the end of elementary school.

His instructional needs are aptly described by Merle Karnes, developer of the Karnes Ameliorative Curriculum (KAC).[6] Karnes's curriculum provides for intensive development to achieve the following goals:

1. A positive self-concept

2. Motivation to learn
3. Cognitive growth with emphasis on language
4. Development of effective information-processing skills
5. Development of perceptual skills
6. Involvement of parents in the educative process

Karnes, who has worked for years as a teacher and is now a professor at the University of Illinois, knows poor children well. Many of her young charges are first and second generation immigrants from Southern farms and villages. She has based the KAC on observations of manifest needs of these years. These observations are listed below.

1. The environment of low-income children is inappropriate for developing the skills, knowledge, and attitudes requisite for success in schools which are oriented to the middle class.
2. Appropriate experiences provided low-income children at an early age can contribute to their optimal development and prevent much of the mental retardation currently prevalent among school-age children from low-income homes.
3. The causes for potential school failure are perceived as residing in the discrepancy between the experiences provided in the environment of the child from a low-income home and those needed to ensure his success in the middle-class oriented school rather than as a deficiency within the child. Thus, the child is viewed as having a positive potential for growth which has been impeded by inappropriate experiences associated with a membership in a low-income family. This assumption rejects the need for a remedial approach which accepts the premise that the child has incapacitating deficiencies and needs highly specialized methods and techniques of instruction because his problems are so complex. When one intervenes at an early age, the specificity of training is not such a problem. The children need to be provided with a curriculum that approximates that of the middle class

child to enable him to be successful in school in subsequent years.

4. The earlier the low-income child and his parents and siblings are involved in an intervention program, the greater the potential for enhancement of the young child's subsequent development. Parents and siblings can acquire improved skills in teaching the young child at home.

5. Since educators do not know precisely what content a child is expected to know in subsequent years, process should be given prime importance with content taking a secondary place.

6. An effective educational program should be comprehensive and give due attention to all facets of the child's development. It should be cognitively based, carefully structured, and individualized. To ensure precise planning to meet individual needs, the teacher must set specific objectives for small groups and for individuals and carefully evaluate the child's progress from day to day.

7. It was felt especially important that a high degree of success for the child was particularly necessary to enhance his self-concept. Positive reinforcement was held to be of prime importance in promoting the learning of the child.

8. Increasing the child's cognitive functioning, especially in language, will enhance his ability to perceive and cope with his environment, thus promoting his socio-affective development. Verbalizations concurrent with multi-sensory presentation would seem to be a requirement for facilitating effective learning. The game format was felt to lend itself to the promotion of cognitive language development.

9. Since language development is highly related to academic success, any program for low-income children must place a high emphasis on language development.

10. A low teacher-pupil ratio (1:5) is a requisite of an early education program for low-income children since promotion of language development is contingent upon the

interactive language behavior between child and adult.

11. The services of the limited number of competent professionals can be extended through the use of paraprofessionals as teachers.

12. A preschool program for the low-income child must be designed to meet the specific needs of groups and individuals but not be so foreign from the educational program in later years that articulation and coordination are impossible.

13. A preschool program for the low-income child must build into its curriculum instruction that will ensure the child's transferring learning in that setting to the regular school program he will be attending in subsequent years. A curriculum which stresses acquisition of information-processing skills would seem to ensure transfer of learning to a greater degree than one which places major stress on acquisition of content.

14. Care must be taken to adequately program for low-income children with high potential, otherwise their full development may be impeded.

15. To ensure the success of a program, there must be a dynamic, on-going, professional growth program for staff. As is true of the program for children, the staff must be perceived as being capable of growth, and individual goals must be set for each staff member toward which he can work to become a more professionally competent person.

16. A model helps organize instruction. Two models seem to particularly lend themselves to this purpose. Since low-income children have inadequate language development, the psycholinguistic theory as represented by the clinical model of the Illinois Test of Psycholinguistic Abilities (ITPA) appeared to afford not only a practical but a theoretically powerful approach. Since the ITPA model does not provide a complete model for the development of intellectual functioning, a more comprehensive model, the Guilford Structure of the Intellect (SI) (Guilford, 1967) appeared to have promise in providing teachers with

guidelines for curriculum development. The SI model was felt to be helpful in ensuring that the teacher provides the children with a broad range of appropriate experiences requiring all types of intellectual operations so as to foster the development of divergent, productive, and evaluative thinking. The SI model complements the ITPA model by extending and expanding the intellectual processing domain.

What Karnes has said as succinctly and vividly as any researcher to date is that the parental and family instructional system of the black middle-class child provides him with a system of language, perception, and typologies for understanding and learning about the world. Successes in learning enable this child to feel good about himself and encourage him to reach out for more learning. The parents, family, and sometimes the schools of needy children provide less of this—the concept that a high-impact program is all about.

Many types of high-impact programs exist.[7] Some excellent programs now in operation are listed in Figure 9. Examples of the excellent results of these programs are the achievement and IQ scores shown in Figure 10. A quite recent addition to the growing list of success stories is the National Advisory Council on the Education of Disadvantaged Children's compilation of 216 outstanding Title I programs. Substantial successes from statewide evaluations of Title I are available from the Connecticut, Michigan, California, and Ohio state departments of education.

The KAC does not state goals of development and then proceed to ignore them in favor of interesting but unfocused classroom activities. For every goal of the KAC, a set of learning experiences that are utterly dependable in enabling the children to realize the goal is provided. The advantages of the structured cognitive high-impact program are several—they focus with a minimum of waste.

Perhaps the most powerful teaching system for black children mangled by poverty is the DISTAR program of Science Research Associates.[8] This program has been refined over the past

FIGURE 9

EFFECTIVE SCHOOL PROGRAMS FOR DISADVANTAGED MINORITY CHILDREN

Name	Place	Number of Students	Curriculum	Test Gains	
				IQ Points	Achievement Score
Banneker School *	Gary, Ind.	1,500	Behavioral Research Laboratories Programmed Instruction.	—	75% of children at or above norm
John H. Finley School	New York, N.Y.	1,000	British Open School program with good phonics teaching and high expectations.	—	Gr. 1 = 2.4 Gr. 4 = 4.8 Gr. 5 = 5.9
P.S. 146	New York, N.Y.	1,200	British Open School program.	—	Gr. 4 = 5.0
Cradle Schools *	Univ. of Wisconsin	40	Infant, preschool, and pre-K training in perception, language, and logic.	Average IQ = 120 Range = 105–135	—
Englemann DISTAR	Univ. of Oregon (Siegfried Englemann)	About 100 schools @ 750 children	Structured phonics, mathematics, and language arts experiences.	Average 100+	Average above national level

SOURCE: National Leadership Institute/Teacher Education, University of Connecticut, Storrs, Connecticut, 1973.
* Completed research and Demonstration Projects.

Program	Location	Enrollment	Description	IQ/Test	Reading Scores
Karnes Ameliorative Curriculum	Univ. of Illinois (Merle Karnes)	About 10 schools @ 750 children	Structured cognitive program stressing learning how to learn and information processing.	105—Program 93—Non-Program	Gr. 1 = 2.0 Gr. 2 = 2.8 Gr. 3 = 3.9
P.S. 11	New York, N.Y.	750	Strong emphasis on phonics, reading, and high expectations for children. Ratio of teachers to children 1:20.	—	42–46% of third graders score fourth grade or higher
Woodland School	Kansas City, Mo.	650	Sullivan Programmed Learning for reading and mathematics. Reading specialist in each school. Heavy phonics emphasis.	—	42–46% of third graders score fourth grade or higher
Ann Street School	Los Angeles, Calif.	450	Sullivan Programmed Reading. Phonics emphasized. Nongraded. Full-time reading specialist.	—	42–46% of third graders score fourth grade or higher
Home Start	Waterloo, Iowa	175	Home study for 2-year-olds plus pre-K starting at four years of age.	100.9 Program 93.0 Non-Program	—
Baltimore Model Early Childhood Program	Baltimore, Md.	500	Piaget-type preschool. Heavy parent participation.	16.06 pre-post testing gain (Md IQ = 100)	—

FIGURE 9 (Continued)
EFFECTIVE SCHOOL PROGRAMS FOR DISADVANTAGED MINORITY CHILDREN

Name	Place	Number of Students	Curriculum	Test Gains	
				IQ Points	Achievement Score
Las Vegas Follow Through	Las Vegas, N. Mex.	395	Englemann DISTAR program. Grades 1–3.	—	Gr. 1 = 1.6 Gr. 2 = 3.1 Gr. 3 = 4.0
Murfreesboro Preschool Development Project	Murfreesboro, Tenn.	355	Mobile classroom for two-hour preschool for 3–4-year-olds.	19.5 prepost	—
Project Conquest	East St. Louis, Ill.	1,089	Remedial reading for grades 1–3.	—	Yearly gain: 1.04 Program .75 Non- Program
P.S. 243 Follow Through	New York, N.Y.	675	Bank Street College Curriculum. Grades K–3.	—	All grades at national test norms
Urban Education Reading Program	Kansas City, Mo.	7,498	Reading specialist in each school promoting individualized and corrective reading.	—	Gr. 1 = 2.7 Gr. 2 = 2.9 Gr. 3 = 3.6
Central Cities Development Center	Fort Worth, Tex.	286	Perception training and language development for 2–5-year-olds.	10 prepost (Md IQ = 100)	—
Diagnostic Reading Clinic	Cleveland, Ohio	532	Daily remedial reading for elementary children.	—	3.65 months gain for each month of instruction

Program	Location	Enrollment	Method	Scores	Results
mental Studies New York University			Emphasis on cognitive functioning. Sequential presentation of stimuli. Learning centers.		Gr. 2 = 2.77
Ypsilanti Perry Preschool Project	Ypsilanti, Mich.	168	Piagetian theory—cognitive objectives and teaching. Home visits to involve parents in educative process.		145 experimental 115 control 195 experimental 112 control Raw scores on second and third grade CAT * Wide Range Achievement Tests Gr. 2 = 4.2 Gr. 3 = 4.9
Project Follow Through	Grand Rapids, Mich.	860	DISTAR	Gr. 2 = 106 Gr. 3 = 103	Reading: Entering Gr. 3 3.0 G.E. † April testing for Gr. 4 4.8 G.E.
Child-Parent Education Centers	Chicago, Ill.	2,100	Direct parent involvement. Elimination of social and health problems. Use of learning materials with specific approaches. Structured programs with feedback available. Direct experiences for skill development. Multiage grouping.		Math: April testing for Gr. 4 4.9 G.E.

* CAT is the California Achievement Test.
† G.E. is grade equivalency.

FIGURE 9 (Continued)
EFFECTIVE SCHOOL PROGRAMS FOR DISADVANTAGED MINORITY CHILDREN

Name	Place	Number of Students	Curriculum	Test Gains	
				IQ Points	Achievement Score
Mother-Child Home Program	Freeport, N.Y.	11 centers in 10 states "graduated" 250 in N.Y.	Home visits that teach mothers how to interact and stimulate their children verbally through the use of books and toys. Children keep toys and materials.	Prepost IQ gains of 19 points on Peabody, Stanford-Binet, and Catell tests; 104 average IQ gains.	
Holy Angels School	Chicago, Ill.	1,300	Strong emphasis on traditional teaching of academic subjects. Heavy phonics and strong discipline.	Scores on standardized tests about the national norm for each grade, scores are above average for Chicago schools.	
Behavior Analysis	Bronx, N.Y. Hopi, Ariz. Indianapolis, Ind. Kansas City, Kans. Meridian, Ill. Northern Cheyenne, Mont. Philadelphia, Pa. Pittsfield, Mass. Portageville, Mo. Trenton, N.J. Waukegan, Ill.	8,000 in 11 school sys.	Behavior Analysis define objectives diagnose motivate through reinforcement teach evaluate	Tests exceed national norms.	

Public School 91	Brooklyn, N.Y.	1,245	Basic skills taught in reading and arithmetic in kindergarten. Reduced teacher-child ratio in early grades. Principal leads program personally.	51.4% of pupils at or above national norm on reading tests.
Learning Centers	Oklahoma City, Okla.	3,000	Remedial reading and math labs. Diagnostic prescriptive teaching mode.	(Scores are mean gain in entire project) *Elementary* Reading 1.3 year gain per school year; Math 1.2 year gain per school year. *Middle School* Reading 1.5 year gain per semester; Math .9 year gain per semester. *High School* Reading .9 year gain per semester
Rooms of Fifteen	St. Louis, Mo.	1,485	Ninety-nine Rooms of Fifteen, which literally refers to classrooms of no more than 15 students, is a Title I program of remedial work in the basic skills of reading, language, and arithmetic.	Average Reading Gain in 10 Months (Spring '71–Spring '72): Gr. 2 = 14.1 Gates-MacGinitie**; Gr. 3 = 15.9; Gr. 4 = 10.9; Gr. 5 = 12.9 ITBS††; Gr. 6 = 12.5

** A reading test developed by H. M. Gates and William MacGinitie and published by the Teachers College Press.

†† ITBS is the Iowa Tested Basic Skills test.

FIGURE 9 (Continued)
EFFECTIVE SCHOOL PROGRAMS FOR DISADVANTAGED MINORITY CHILDREN

Name	Place	Number of Students	Curriculum	Test Gains	
				IQ Points	Achievement Score
Reading Improvement Teams	St. Louis, Mo.	13,000	The RIT, composed of the principal, reading assistant, remedial reading teacher, reading aide, and ten classroom teachers, works as a team with students who have the most severe reading problems in 66 Title I schools.		Gr. 1 = 10.1 Gates-MacGinitie Gr. 2 = 14.6 Gr. 3 = 16.6 Gr. 4 = 9.2 Gr. 5 = 11.6 Gr. 6 = 10.2 ITBS Gr. 7 = 10.9 Gr. 8 = 10.1

SUMMARY

Number of Programs — 29
Number of School Systems — 126 (plus two universities)
Number of Children — 131,179 (approximate)
Average IQ Produced — 100+
Average Grade Level Produced — National test norms met or exceeded for each program

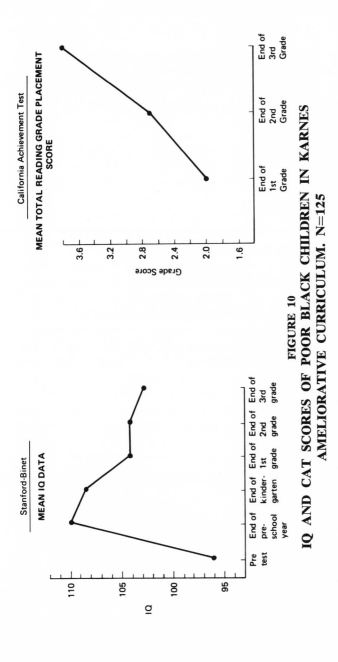

FIGURE 10

IQ AND CAT SCORES OF POOR BLACK CHILDREN IN KARNES AMELIORATIVE CURRICULUM. N=125

FOR DISADVANTAGED MINORITY CHILDREN

SOURCE: Merle Karnes, *Structured Cognitive Approach for Educating Young Children: Report of a Successful Program* (Technical Bulletin, National Leadership Institute/Teacher Education, University of Connecticut, 1972).

fifteen years by Siegfried Englemann of the University of Oregon. DISTAR is an acronym for Direct Instruction in Arithmetic and Reading. For those over the age of forty, DISTAR is reminiscent of the type of reading and arithmetic learned in their grade schools. DISTAR is far more, however, although the program concentrates on basics like phonics instruction and good scope and solid sequence planning. The disasters of many of the new experimental programs are based on alarming departures from these basics. George Weber of the Council for Basic Education has noted that the middle-class child who has been prepped extensively in homes and preschools will teach himself phonics, for example, but others without this preparation are not able to teach themselves and become casualties in the struggle to break the reading code.

DISTAR has been developed to overcome several hazards poor black children encounter in their schools. Beginning with scope and sequence, DISTAR's reading program teaches 32 word sounds, full sentence reading, and language arts skills in 26 areas, in 159 reading and 180 language (thirty-minute) lessons in the first year. The lessons are all structured and are contained in booklets. The responses of both teachers and pupils are spelled out. Formative tests are included that enable teachers quickly to begin students at the proper sequence as indicated by their level of development. Criterion tests are included that enable teachers quickly to ascertain mastery for *every* child.

Contrast this carefully planned sequence with the disarray presented in Jonathan Kozol's *Death At An Early Age*.[9] Each of the six teachers who were assigned to one unfortunate class in a school term taught whatever she could or felt inclined to teach to the poor, confused children.

One cannot leave a discussion of high-impact programs without calling attention to the Chicago Child-Parent Centers, one of the biggest success stories in this arena. CCPCs are a network of eleven centers involving 2,100 children and their parents. The program enrolls children from three to nine years old in carefully planned learning experiences and works with parents to bolster this learning. CCPC graduates score above national levels on their fourth and fifth grade tests. A full description of the CCPC program is included in Appendix B.

Figures 11 and 12 are scope and sequence charts for first-year DISTAR reading and language arts.

Home Start and Cradle Schools

To lessen the burden of school-based amelioration, a home-based program to assist parents in the home and family curriculum is desirable for poor black children. The Office of Child Development has initiated a rather broad program entitled Home Start that is structured in this vein. A parent-child center program is also operating in a small (thirty-five communities) number of locations.

Home Starts can either be teacher-based or parent-based. Rick Heber's highly successful "cradle schools" are a good example of the former, while the Waterloo, Iowa, program is a fine example of the latter.[10]

Heber began his program in 1965 and probably has the most voluminous longitudinal data ever collected on intensive infant and child development. Operating in the worst census income and housing tract in Milwaukee, Heber enrolled forty infants in cradle schools at five days of age. Until age two, each child had a personal teacher who visited and played with him for several hours each day, expertly offering the psychophysical stimulation so vitally necessary for proper development of perception and language. Important to note is that about one-half of an individual's basic intellectual development takes place in these first two or three years and that the key is the development of habitual and effective methods of sensing and organizing the environment. This sensing and organizing requires a perceptual typology system that, in turn, requires a language system to undergird it.

At around age two, Heber moved the children into small groups of ten with a teacher and one or more paraprofessionals for each group. The children are now in kindergarten and first

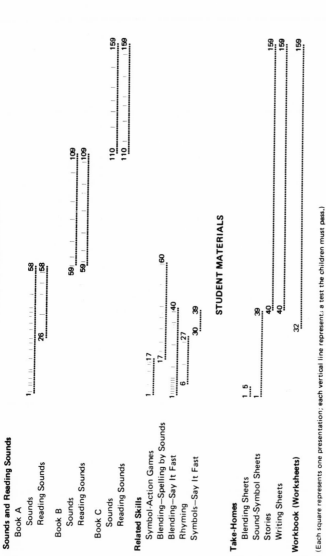

TEACHER PRESENTATIONS

Sounds and Reading Sounds

Book A
Sounds
Reading Sounds

Book B
Sounds
Reading Sounds

Book C
Sounds
Reading Sounds

Related Skills

Symbol-Action Games
Blending—Spelling by Sounds
Blending—Say It Fast
Rhyming
Symbols—Say It Fast

STUDENT MATERIALS

Take-Homes

Blending Sheets
Sound-Symbol Sheets
Stories
Writing Sheets

Workbook (Worksheets)

(Each square represents one presentation; each vertical line represents a test the children must pass.)

FIGURE 11

DISTAR READING I SCOPE AND SEQUENCE CHART

SOURCE: *DISTAR* ™ *READING I*, Teacher's Guide by Siegfried Engelmann and Elaine C. Bruner.

SCOPE AND SEQUENCE CHART

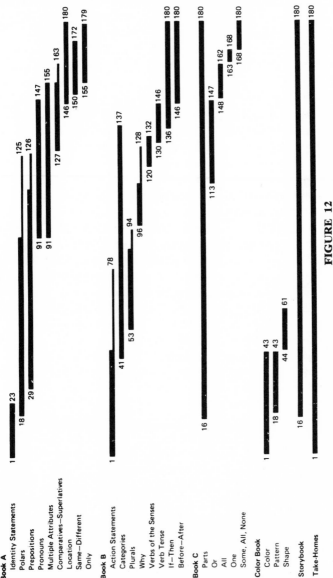

FIGURE 12

SCOPE AND SEQUENCE CHART

SOURCE: *DISTAR* ™ *LANGUAGE* I, Teacher's Guide by Siegfried Engelmann and Elaine C. Bruner.

grade. The children talk freely among themselves, make up stories and tell them, play teacher, learn reading at a rapid rate, and are whizzes at test passing. The average IQ in the group is 120 with a range of 105–135.

The Waterloo Home Start program is an example of a parent-based program. Taking three years, the program guides a child and his parent(s) through two years of home enrichment, followed by a 2½-hour classroom experience five days a week in the prekindergarten year.[11] During these three years, the focus continues to be facilitating learning within the home. In the project, educational procedures are being individualized, using results from the Learning Readiness Systems (LRS) Seriation Test. Throughout the three-year period, an achievement-oriented test will be administered at six-month intervals to enable the home visitor to individualize educational procedures employed within the home. Paid aides and staff members (speech consultant, home economist—depending upon need) visit homes to improve parent-child interaction, including the selection of educational toys for stimulating development within the home. Family-oriented activities are discussed in crafts and homemaking classes taught by a home economist. Home Start provides fewer direct services and requires more parent initiative. Mothers come to the Home Start center to pick up instructional materials. Three consultants work with mothers to aid them in teaching their children. Various community agencies also work with the project to provide services for the children and families of both groups.

Black children enrolled in Waterloo Home Start average 101 on IQ tests as compared to 92 for similar children not enrolled. Follow-up of students in the schools shows that they are learning at an average or above average rate.

Home Starts and cradle schools can be operated by schools as well as by community groups. The cost is high for teacher-based programs (about $2,500 per child) and nominal for parent-based (about $1,000 per child), but any reasonable investment at this age saves thousands of dollars in remedial work and lost tax revenues from decreased productivity of under-educated workers.

Community-Based Programs

Some of the more effective programs to spur achievement in depressed areas have involved strong leadership by black superintendents who rallied parental energies. Samuel Shephard of St. Louis is a good case in point with the remarkable successes of the Banneker district schools of the late 1950s and early 1960s. Robert Wheeler of Kansas City is another fine example, and Wilson Riles and John Porter offered the same type of leadership as commissioners of education for California and Michigan. These two states, for example, boast the most effective Title I programs in the nation.

Working-class neighborhoods, black and white, are outdoor, mechanistic cultures and will have to make a special effort to find time for the reading activities necessary to develop these skills at the same rate as children of clerks and better-educated parents. Working-class children also put in an inordinate amount of time perfecting sports skills.

The simple fact, therefore, is that many of the reading deficits in these communities can be traced to the lack of reading on the part of the children. Children must bounce the ball on the floor a requisite number of times to become good basketball players and they must read a certain volume of pages of increasing difficulty to become good readers. The form is stringent with no substitutions. Community-based academic programs are quite simple but require large amounts of energy and drive on the part of administrators. Dr. Shephard addressed 325 parent groups in the first year of his program. His message was simple and direct: Children in the twenty-two-school Banneker district must put in more time on reading and math. He was counting on the parents to get this job done. He followed this challenge with charts on test score progress of the district and visuals on how to reward (or punish) the child in the drive for less street, sports, TV, and mechanical time and more reading and math.

Shephard also worked with his teachers and focused their energies on the problem of better test scores. Courses of study were checked to make sure teachers were not teaching one thing and the testers testing another. Effective administration of tests was stressed. Precautions necessary for minority children were taken.

More and more black administrators will be at the helm in city schools, and they can rally parents in community-based achievement drives in which whites would surely fail or where they would lack the initiative and interest in the first place. Reading summers, district competition, parents as homework supervisors, and a vast array of other projects are possible under hard-driving black administrators. White universities that want to help black communities can surely make a contribution by reducing the amount of money directed toward urban semesters, studies of the black community, and other nostrums and increasing recruitment and scholarship programs to train the type of black administrators needed. One Robert Wheeler is worth ten gaggles of sophomores from suburban communities spending university money to "study the culture of poverty."

However, a demurrer must be added. The testing apparatus of the schools must be changed for the sake of quality education for both blacks and whites. Community-based programs must take this step into consideration as they set their goals and measure their results. Fifty percent of the children in normative-based testing will always wind up below the mean, and this group will usually contain the majority of the future plumbers, electricians, mechanics, and metals fabricators. If mechanistic youngsters become involved in a test race, how will the mechanical skills be developed? A better method of measurement would be the ratio of months gained on tests to months taught with grade level discarded. If a district can report that the average child made 1.0 months gain for each month taught, a satisfactory rate of progress is being maintained. The children are spared the suburban neurosis in which parents become hysterical if the district cannot report that the children are two grades above the median. Hopefully, the locator-criterion tests discussed throughout the book will spread even more rapidly, and tests will become a part of the solution to American educational problems instead of continuing to be a part of the problem.

High-School Programs for Poor Black Youth

As noted earlier, black high-school persistence has been the success story of the past decade. High-school graduation rates jumped from 36 to 62 percent during this period. Young black adults pulled very nearly abreast of their counterparts in years of schooling completed (12.1 to 12.4 years).

If black graduation rates are to climb to the 80 percent targeted for 1980 and if most blacks are to be graduated from high school in 1999, black adolescents in severely depressed areas must be afforded intensive, insightful, and inventive programs to help them stay with their work till graduation.

Poor blacks leave school early much for the same reasons as poor whites: money is needed; poverty places strains on family life; serene routines necessary for study are unavailable. In addition, black adolescents carry the added burden of racism, which uses up an inordinate amount of mental and social energy and generates a great uncertainty about whether a high-school diploma will be useful at all in the marketplace. Ten months after the graduation of a Washington, D.C., senior class, for example, 35 percent of its members were still looking for jobs.

A public-service program guaranteeing a $5,000 job to each high-school graduate will do far more than any school program one can devise for this group. Schools have the responsibility to make this need clear to politicians and industrialists. An error in the strategies of the past has been the overdependence on education alone to alleviate poverty. The schools have said that if a youth were qualified and certified by their diplomas, he would get a good job. Black youths are acutely aware that this may not always be true. In the end, blame is laid at the feet of the school for not qualifying youngsters who see no payoff in being qualified in the first place.

One should not be surprised then to find that work-study programs that enable youth to simultaneously fend off the dislocations and disarray of poverty to some extent, to learn both job and college preparatory skills, and to make job and college entrance connections are highly effective in raising the graduation rates in depressed areas. This type of work-study program is not to be confused with vocational education. Vocational education has many problems and will be discussed later in this book.

School systems might well generate a quantum jump in high-school graduation rates by developing a wide variety of work-study opportunities for students. Where business and industry are too feeble or too bigoted to make a place for black youngsters from poor families, the federal government should provide funds for jobs with public-service agencies to be shared on a rotating basis by students. For example, a group of ten students might be assigned for the first semester of the school year to work at a variety of tasks in a city tax department's data-processing facility. The students might take their English and mathematics classes for this semester by attending two-hour classes twice a week in the evening adult-education program of the school. During the second semester, the children would put in a full semester at school and another group of ten would come to data processing. In the summers, both groups would work and take the two courses omitted during their work semesters. With a guaranteed job at the end of high school, almost all of these young people would graduate. Upon graduation, hopefully many of the students would be prepared academically, financially, and psychologically for college and others would be well prepared and well connected for the world of work.

One cannot stress the necessity of using work-study and every other available device for preparing large numbers of poor black youth for college. Aside from the moral aspects of making this effort, the simple fact exists that the black demography demands it. Middle-class blacks, unlike whites, do not replace themselves. The birth rate of the middle class, which traditionally sends almost all of its children to college and which produces the substantial share of professionally trained blacks, is 1.6 children per family. Middle-class whites averaged 2.6 in 1969—although the drive toward zero population growth is depressing this figure sharply. The replacement requirement is 2.11 children per family.

A comprehensive black strategy for black-white comparability in jobs will require an increase in the birth rate of the black middle class, a birth rate for black poor families that allows for full development of the children, and a concentrated effort to send a larger proportion of poor youths to college and/or into high-paying jobs and businesses than whites. Failure to do at least the first and the latter will result in a constant struggle in the black community to provide leadership and professional services for its people. More is said on this concept in Chapter 7.

Cooperative-education programs have been in existence for many years and have been highly successful. According to the official brochure, 60 percent of the six thousand New York City Co-op students find jobs where they did their training. The Committee on Labor and Public Welfare of the U.S. Senate states, "The Part-time Cooperative Plan is undoubtedly the best program we have in vocational education. It consistently yields high placement records, high employment stability, and high job satisfaction." [12]

The term *cooperative education* can mean several things. In this book, the term will refer to programs set up on a work-study basis. The student's academic work will be combined with work experience away from the school setting. This separation would be physical only. A cooperative-education program is a total learning experience linking theory with practice.

Statistics at the end of 1971 showed 379,840 students in cooperative-education programs. Another 28,726 pupils were involved in work-study programs where their work experience was not necessarily connected with their school work.

A successful cooperative-education program is very difficult to establish. However, such a program has the potential of being a very meaningful learning experience. Cooperative education presents an alternative to traditional forms of education that are turning kids off. One major plus of a well-run cooperative-education program is the motivation to learn sparked in the participants. Possibly for the first time in their school careers, students can see a link between their school theories and the outside world.

Summer Enrichment Programs

Some of the most effective programs for preparing poor black youth for college have been the wide variety of summer enrichment schools for poor youth. The most widely known is the Upward Bound program established by the Office of Economic Opportunity (OEO) and now operated by the U.S. Office of Education. Starting with tenth graders, this program brings students to college campuses for a summer of extra work and counseling. Teams are recruited from high schools and Upward Bound personnel work with these young people during the school year. The graduate of Upward Bound is guided into the proper channels for student scholarships and aid and is well acclimated to college life. The Bureau of Higher Education of the USOE compiled a remarkable list of enrollment figures in 1972 showing successes of Upward Bound graduates in college matriculation. Graduates of the Summer Program at the University of Connecticut match university averages in college competition according to a June, 1973, report of the dean of students. Graduates of this program are now enrolled in studies at Yale University Law School and Stanford University Graduate School.

The National Science Foundation sponsors a number of summer programs for students. Talented black students have benefitted from this activity, especially in the South. An expansion of this program is desirable, or at least an expansion of black participation in it.

Preparatory Schools

The best method for adding to the preparation of poor youths who are able to succeed in college is the preparatory school—a time-honored method of strengthening high-school graduates of all classes and incomes. Bullis Preparatory School in Washington, D.C., is an example of effective preparation for rigorous curricula. Bullis prepares large numbers of students for the U.S.

Naval Academy. The U.S. Air Force Academy has its own preparatory school located on the campus. Two hundred fifty students are enrolled for a year of mind-bending work that sets students up well for the curricula of the academy.

Harlem Prep and Newark Prep have outstanding records for preparing needy black youths for college. Working under the aegis of the Urban League, these two schools have sent nearly five hundred needy black youths through their schools. All were admitted to college and all succeeded in college.

Black youths would benefit greatly from an expansion of preparatory-school operations. Creative efforts to bring this expansion about would swell the ranks of talented youth from depressed communities.

The U.S. Navy has established a preparatory school for disadvantaged black youngsters on its San Diego base. The program's acronym is Boost. The program offers an all-expenses-paid year of solid preparation for one hundred high-school graduates who are interested in competing for slots at the Naval Academy. All of these young men will probably enter some college if not the Naval Academy. All will probably succeed because of this added maturity and preparation. This program costs less than $200,000 a year and is a good model for the type of expansion needed.

Some of the black colleges might consider re-entry into the preparatory field. Some of the strongest black professionals have come out of the old prep schools once operated by such institutions as Wilberforce University in Ohio and Hampton Institute in Virginia. In a broad talent development effort, the federal government might very well finance such efforts.

Many federal departments could operate preparatory schools for black youth in their far-flung schools and colleges. The U.S. Department of Agriculture's Graduate School and the Army Officer Candidate School all operate college-level and could easily add preparatory schools to increase the academic strengths of black youth. Each institution might set up a school and find money for stipends and room and board for 250 students.

A goal of enrolling 25,000 black preparatory students each year might be quite reasonable. This enrollment would represent

20 percent of the top 125,000 black eighteen-year-olds each year, who in turn represent the top 25 percent of the 500,000 black eighteen-year-olds. The 25,000 prep-school graduates would represent 10 percent of the expected 250,000 or so black freshmen on college and university campuses in 1980.

If fifty black colleges enrolled 12,500 of the students and federal schools the other 12,500, the goal of 25,000 prep students would be exceeded as states and colleges and corporations began to see the value of this approach.

Variations of preparatory schools might be an "academy college" that offers a highly individualized curriculum and as much college work as possible. By using the College Level Examination Program (CLEP) measurements of Educational Testing Service, students could enter an academy college and be placed two years later at a comfortable level in the sophomore class of most colleges in the country.

Programs for Gifted Black Children

William Moore likes to tell the story of his first contact with the American school system. Moore was taken by his mother to the first-grade teacher in his neighborhood school in St. Louis in a depressed area around Pine and Labadie streets. On the first day a large white man from the central office came to his room and took Moore and the others, in small groups, to a hall closet where he was given an IQ test. The man returned the confused children to their room, gathered his test sheets from the closet, and went back to the central office. A month later, Moore's teacher received his test results and confronted Moore with the bad news: the test predictions, corroborated by her own impressions after a month of working with Moore, were that he would never finish high school. Moore went on to become a college president in Seattle, Washington. He finished his Ph.D. in psychology before the age of thirty and has written two books and a raft of articles. This anecdote epitomizes as well as any the actual mangling of talent by grinding poverty and bad schools. Run-of-the-mill geniuses would never have climbed out of a depressed area in St. Louis in the 1940s and many cannot climb out today for lack of good common-sense programs to develop gifted disadvantaged black children.

Black communities must insist that schools use more effective methods of identifying gifted talent and must combine with the schools in vigorous efforts to develop this talent.

Clifford Stallings, of United States International University in San Diego, is a psychologist who is an expert on gifted disadvantaged children. He has written a treatise on identifying and developing these children, which should be valuable to any school or community group attempting to assure full development of the talents of its gifted black children.[13]

Stallings suggests a combination of teacher observation and new environment-based tests as methods of identifying talented black children in depressed areas. Children who recognize similarities, discern differences, and generalize from the two are the children to watch, according to Stallings. He urges teachers to make their own environmental tests to identify unusual talent. Recall of street signs in a ten-block radius will surface children with genius in this area, as will recall of types of automobiles parked on the street, the mosaic of shop and store signs, and embellishment of details (i.e., color, type of wheels, and functions).

Stallings notes that teachers must be alert to confusion caused by the distinctive and expressive language of metropolitan black children. Often children will find themselves trapped between double meanings of the same word. Simple words like *cool, together, rap, dig, lay, swing, gig,* and *bread* all have dual meanings in the expressive language of the gifted metropolitan child, and teachers must recognize this bilinguality and build upon it.

William Labov, the linguist, describes the dilemma of school authorities in dealing with black vernacular. Labov, in an article in *The Atlantic* entitled, "Black Intelligence and Academic Ignorance," puts his finger on the root cause of this dilemma.[14] The cause rests in the overvaluing of lengthy verbal abstractions and the undervaluing of succinct encapsulation by the American middle class. The former is often mistaken for intelligence, Labov points out, although many children and adults ramble on and spin such a web of abstractions and qualifications that teachers, parents, and employers often despair of ever getting them to come to grips with the heart of a problem.

Labov notes that a more valid test of ability is silent sorting of factors in a difficult problem and short verbal encapsulation of both the problem and its solution. He points out that the Southern heritage of most black ghetto dwellers fits them well for this sort of analysis. Indeed, lengthy, verbal abstractions are discouraged in the homes of black working people. A child is taught to be brief, direct, honest, and to the point. As Labov points out, he uses vivid black vernacular to meet these requirements.

Teachers must recognize this form of derring-do, identify those children with unusual abilities in analysis and encapsulation, and work to develop their gifts in a bilingual setting. A metropolitan child who responds to a discussion of the efficacy of antipoverty efforts by noting that "there ain't no question; people dig Headstart and all but a really cool scene is if the government make some gigs available to the people or lays some bread on them" has analyzed a difficult problem, developed an accurate, short reply, and used an expressive language system to present it. Government planners use reams of paper to try to make the same point clear to politicians and their strategists; educational and social programs are appreciated by poor people, but an effective addition to antipoverty efforts would be the provision of jobs for the unemployed or the provision of income to these families. The child who makes these connections immediately and uses BEV (Black English Vernacular) to express them vividly has gifts that should be developed. He can learn an academic language, standard grammar, and syntax. If teachers understand the mental processes involved, appreciate the cultural heritages of these processes and the language used to express them, he could move into law, medicine, and other areas. The problem is talent conservation and development in unique cultural settings.

Stallings also urges the close observation of leadership types in the black metropolitan school or other settings and the development of children with special penchants for organization.

One might question the need for more charismatic, spell-binding politicians in the black community and the point might be well made. However, a large cadre of different types of organizers will be needed in the future. Huge numbers of corporate-type leaders will be needed in the future for black entrepreneurism, manning the educational systems, and city governments. The new leader is going to be adroit at developing systems that deliver and at the astute application of human and other resources to the successful operations of these systems.

Stallings notes that metropolitan children with unusual capabilities for organizing playground activities, getting consensus in group work, organizing the business affairs of the class, and taking charge in emergencies have talents of organization that should be developed. This child will form a corporation twenty years later, float bonds, raise capital, produce a product, market it and make jobs, or keep city government on an even keel. In many cases, this child will also have unusual analytical and encapsulation skills coupled with good coordination and physical skills.

The programs that can be developed for gifted black children and youth are limited only by the creativity of the teachers and administrators involved. A basic objective should be the development of day-to-day routines within which the minds of these children will have full rein, where the children do not have to wait for the teacher to teach in order for them to learn, where advanced materials are at the fingertips of the children, and where outside resources are used to challenge their minds.

The gifted disadvantaged black child will flourish best in nongraded elementary schools and collegiate or open-scheduled high schools with plenty of access to community resources. Notably, a program labeled gifted is not necessary here and may even be counterproductive. Black culture is essentially a sharing culture—a culture that holds its achievers dear but considers inordinate attention to this sort of thing as bad taste. Black genius is correctly viewed as a community asset, something that all the community will willingly sacrifice to develop and that brings joy and pride to the community. Labeling children and programs gifted in black schools may rip up this delicate fabric.

James Jones, age six and ranking among the top thinkers and/or organizers to come to Banneker School over the years, might be spotted by his teachers or his environment tests in the first month at school. Jim would be assigned to tutor his class-mates, given early use of the Polaroid camera for development of picture stories, asked to do special reports, given leadership roles in groups, and put in touch with special resource people in various areas.

As Jim moved through the school, he would have done per-haps three times as much cognitive work as the average child in school and come in contact with five times as many gifted adults who would stretch his mind. The latter aspect is a place where gifted retired people in the community can make themselves useful. Writers, artists, politicians, inventors, scientists, and other intellectuals would be invited to the school to hold semi-nars, serve as artists-in-residence, and in myriad ways challenge Jim and his other gifted black colleagues.

Corporations and government agencies might give released time to their personnel to work with Jim on organizational structures, mathematics, or the sciences. One of the more suc-cessful ghetto programs in mathematics is the SEEDS program in which IBM and Westinghouse mathematicians teach theorems to elementary-school children.

If leadership were his forte, Jim should be able to participate in a wide variety of leadership roles in high school. If teachers and administrators are not careful, the integrated school might falter in the area of black leadership development. If special efforts are not made, the integrated school may break down. Jim must participate in student-exchange programs, go to Spain with the Spanish club, participate in Boys' State, organize the senior-class trip to Washington, and be eligible for the leading role in the class play. Hopefully, if science is Jim's forte, he will be guided into summer National Science Foundation institutes and afforded experiences in laboratories of local industry and colleges. Again, the integrated school will require work. Poor black male adolescents in these schools are not afforded experi-ences of this magnitude with the possible exception of athletics.

If the boy cannot enhance the reputation of the school's coach, athletics, too, is a limited area.

Hopefully, the nation can rally its resources to work with the 1.5 million or so black children and youth with special gifts and talents. About one-half of these young people are poor. Full development of their abilities and full benefits of their talents to the black community and the nation depend heavily on the abilities of educators to spot unusual talent in poor settings, celebrate the unique expressions and manifestations of this talent, and organize programs to develop it.

Vocational and Technical Education

Vocational and technical education is a problem area for both black and white students, but it affects poor black youth quite harshly.

First, black students are overrepresented in vocational education. Education in this area has not come too far since the time of Booker T. Washington, it seems. This problem is especially true for the children of the five million blacks who came to Northern and Western cities during the last three decades as a result of the revolution in Southern agriculture, caused in part, ironically, by a black scientist's research on soybeans and peanuts. Exact figures are not available regarding black enrollment in vocational education, but a report of the National Association of Manufacturers (NAM) notes that four million students are enrolled and a large number of these are children of newcomers from the South.[15] "Training schools" in the South have always stressed vocational agriculture, mechanical arts, and home economics for both black and white students.

Good vocational and technical education could serve large numbers of black and white students well. If, for example, students could enter a $6,000-per-year job in electricity, data processing, mechanics, construction, or office machines upon graduation and work their way up the income ladder, more students would opt from the scramble for the college degree in a rapidly overcrowding job market situation.

In the foreseeable future, students with college educations will comprise 25 percent or less of the labor force. Further, many students are wondering whether it isn't better to be an $18,000-a-year plasterer than a $9,000-a-year accountant. Society is also beginning to wonder. A widely publicized news item in the spring of 1972 described the graduation of nearly eight hundred students from a college in a city in the upper Midwest that could not boast of a single licensed plumber.

Overrepresentation of poor black youth in vocational programs could be beneficial, but first, an analysis of what they are enrolling into would clarify many things regarding the wisdom of this course of action. New light is also thrown on black dropout rates in high school and black achievement on standardized tests in studies such as the Coleman Report, a massive study of school achievement sponsored by the U.S. Office of Education, which did not control for such overrepresentation.

Vocational education is in trouble in many places. According to a report by the National Association of Manufacturers, which is cited at length below, only 50 percent of vocational-education graduates find jobs related to their training. Thirty-seven percent were enrolled in home economics or agriculture, six times more than the projected need will be. Only 12 percent were studying trades and industry, although one-third of the projected job market for the future will be in these areas. The costs of vocational education is $1,000 to $1,500 higher than average per-pupil costs in any given locality. Through a rapid shift, the majority of vocational students come from poverty families. In light of the above statistics, one needn't wonder why the dropout rate of vocational students is 45 percent—seven times higher than the dropout average for the nation. An accompanying shift in emphasis on high-impact academic programs designed to compensate for this movement has not been noted.

In light of this above information (that the dropout rate of vocational students is 45 percent, seven times higher than the dropout average for the nation), why these students have below average verbal and mathematical scores on standardized tests should not be puzzling.

Reconsideration should be given the Coleman Report (*Equality of Educational Opportunity*).[16] Comparisons of 600,000 students were made, and as expected, black high-school students scored lower than white high-school students. But Coleman, a Johns Hopkins sociologist with a seemingly limited grasp of how schools work and how black society is organized, failed to control either for social class or for enrollment by curriculum. A. J. Mayeske of the U.S. Office of Education finally reworked Coleman's data, grouping according to social class. Mayeske's data showed little if any difference in test scores.[17] A grouping according to curriculum enrollment (vocational-academic) would probably yield the same results.

The Coleman affair is a textbook example of how well-meaning whites manage to deepen stereotypes about blacks with inaccurate research originally designed to do good. The Coleman Report was released in 1965. Mayeske did not read his paper correcting these errors until 1971. Six years of writing and rewriting of the Coleman data fixed these inaccuracies firmly in the minds of many people.

Coleman's data—or rather Mayeske's corrections—are useful, however, in pointing the way toward improvements in vocational education in relation to black students. First, necessity calls for the liberation of many black students from vocational curricula. Many improvements are needed in the guidance offices in this respect. A constant struggle exists on the part of many blacks in integrated schools, seemingly to avoid being dumped into vocational curricula that prepare them for nothing and lead to no place.

Some of the strongest criticism related to this problem was leveled by R. D. Russell in an article in a special issue of the *Personnel and Guidance Journal*. Russell, who is a counselor, begins as follows:

In the ensuing years my involvement in education has brought me in direct contact with hundreds of young black high school and college students and dropouts from both—who live and attend schools in various cities and suburbs. *I have yet to encounter one black student who had anything positive to say about his high-school guidance experience!* [18]

Russell goes on to note that students are alarmingly bitter about their counselors and that their most frequent criticism involves dumping of black students into bad vocational curricula and denial of access to more meaningful programs in the school. Once relegated to nonacademic programs, one student told Russell, "It's like they lock you in and throw away the key."

Russell noted that the situation seems most pronounced in the Northern integrated school. He points out that in fifteen years of working with black high-school and college students in segregated systems in the South, he had never heard a black student denounce a counselor for mangling his hopes and aspirations by denouncing his goals as unrealistic and unattainable and then shunting him into a feeble vocational-education curriculum.

With the new student-assistance program for college students, guidance counselors have no excuse for telling poor black youths they are being unrealistic to aspire to college and then shunting them into vocational curricula. The new program guarantees $1,400 a year to every student for college enrollment. This one provision alone should substantially lower the number of black students enrolled in substandard vocational programs.

Black students, parents, and community groups have a choice to make here. Given a good vocational program such as the work-study programs described earlier, substantial numbers of students should enroll. Where instruction is bad and placement in jobs is bad, *no* black students enroll. According to the NAM, these students would be better off taking an academic course and presenting themselves to industry as apt, well-educated, and highly trainable workers. According to NAM, many firms have become completely disillusioned with vocational programs and have established their own programs to train and educate high-school graduates and many dropouts.

Again, guiding more poor black students into college-bound programs and guiding future industrial workers into academic programs will do wonders for high-school retention rates and for levels of achievement of black students in this stratum.

Second, a concerted effort must be made to improve both the technical and academic training of young people still enrolled in vocational programs. The following is the essence of the recommendations NAM set for the revamping of vocational programs.[19]

1. Work-study programs would be expanded with provisions for the maintenance of high quality in these programs.
2. An effort to integrate a high quality of academic work with the vocational curriculum would be made. Here the context and object lessons of mathematics and science would be based largely on needs for this information in the shops. Geometry problems, for example, would be the computation of cubic inches of cylinder displacement, angles of dwell of ignition points, and so on.
3. More general preindustrial education would be offered rather than concentration and perhaps overspecializing in one trade.
4. A larger number of students would enroll in trades and industry education where one-third of the future jobs will be.
5. Performance contracts with industry for provision of occupational-training components would be expanded.
6. Systematic methods of evaluating programs would be developed and required.
7. Schools, business, and industry would sit down in each community, analyze worker needs in all areas on a long-range (twenty-year) basis, and develop a variety of school and school-industrial programs to provide these workers.

A good example of school-industry-business planning was developed in the Wilmington, Delaware, program that utilized cooperative work-study extensively.

A program that utilizes both work-study and a school-industry-business-planned technical center is operated by the

Norfolk, Virginia, public schools. Students attend a technical center built with federal funds from the Vocational Education Act of 1963. Students attend for a half day and are bused to their high schools for regular academic curricula and for cocurricular activities. Twenty technical occupations are taught. All were developed by advisory committees from a school-business-industry-union council. All guarantee placement upon graduation and all are subject to phase-out and replacement by higher-demand occupations when or if their work-force demands lessen.

Far too many black high-school students have been shunted into a program that itself is in serious trouble. Many black students must be guided from this program. Other young adults must avoid being trapped in the vocational-education dead end. Every effort must be made to expand effective programs of vocational education. Every effort must be made also to phase out ineffective programs and use the money for smaller classes and high-impact academic programs to enable black youth to compete more equitably at the industrial hiring gates and training programs.

Vocational education has been a hidden Achilles' heel for black education. The vocational program enrolls three times more than its share of these young people, offers perhaps five times less academic rigor to the students than it should, offers obsolete and substandard training for a job that doesn't exist, and serves as a dropout hatch for one-half or more of the blacks enrolled. Every dismal statistic on black retention, attrition, and achievement of black youth will find at least a partial home laid at the feet of vocational education. Change here is long overdue.

Special Education

A final area of education, one that suffers from some disarray and brings untold misery to black children, is special education. Assignment to special-education classes is several times higher for black than for white children, and a huge proportion of this assignment is based on erroneous testing. Quality education for blacks can never be a reality if large numbers of these children are receiving watered-down curricula and instruction in these classes.

Fortunately for black children, special education is in a state of flux about both misplacement of children and lack of rigor in curricula. Witness, for example, the words of Lloyd Dunn, one of the respected leaders in the special-education movement:

> I have loyally supported and promoted special classes for the educable mentally retarded for most of the last twenty years, but with growing disaffection. In my view, much of our past and present practices are morally and education-ally wrong. We have been living at the mercy of general educators who have referred their problems to us, and we have been generally ill prepared and ineffective in educat-ing them. Let us stop being pressured into continuing and expanding a special education program that we know now to be unjustifiable for many of the children we are dedi-cated to serve. . . . I submit that much of what we have attempted to do for exceptional children has been just as ineffective as have been the efforts of general educators. In some cases I submit that we have been even less effec-tive than the general educator has. Research data will be explicated to support this belief. In no way am I suggesting that we have done what we have in a spirit of malice toward the exceptional child—far from it. I am suggesting that we have been quite sincere in our efforts but equally as naive in terms of improving education for exceptional children.[20]

On the problems of misplacement, Jane Mercer's project should be studied. Mercer indicates bluntly:

> Studies dating back to the 1930s have repeatedly demon-strated the cultural biases inherent in IQ tests and other standardized achievement measures. Yet, in spite of these studies, clinicians have continued to interpret children's performance on these tests as if there were no cultural biases and have never systematically taken socio-cultural

differences into account when interpreting the meaning of a particular child's score. Consequently, we find many children in classes for the mentally retarded whose adaptive behavior, in nonacademic settings, clearly demonstrates that their problems are school-specific and that they are not comprehensively incompetent.[21]

Minorities are also recognizing this problem and have taken important steps to attempt to ameliorate the situation. More than twenty class-action suits have been filed against school units in efforts to force school districts to cease and desist in faulty testing and placement of minority children in classes for the retarded. Further, California legislators, a bellwether group, have worked on at least six pieces of legislation designed to bring some order to a bad situation.

A full discussion of this legislation and legal action is included in Chapter 7. Special education can be reformed to better serve black—and white—children.

First, IQ tests should be eliminated from schools. These tests already have been eliminated in an ever-growing number of school districts. Some of the most astute leaders, scientists, and men and women of letters came through school systems without IQ testing. Schools will operate more efficiently without these measures.

Second, a determination should be made that all but the most severely retarded children are going to stay in the regular classroom. The need for labeling and dumping is thereby eliminated.

Third, criterion-referenced testing as propounded by Henry Dyer, the past Executive Vice President of the Educational Testing Service, and others should replace normative-based achievement testing. Normative-based tests "race" children by comparing them to teach other. Criterion tests compare their progress in relation to clear standards of mastery.

Fourth, Piagetian programs should be the rule rather than the exception in primary education. The school ascertains the level of development of every child and uses the school program to maximize this development. Child-racing is eliminated. (Jean

Piaget, the Swiss theorist, has affected greatly American schools with his programmed emphasis on stages of children's learning. More needs to be done in this area.)

Fifth, culture-specific tests should be developed and used in the few cases where intensive diagnosis is needed. The manipulation of familiar symbols assures more accuracy in diagnosis and eliminates language and geography as factors. A Mississippi Delta child might be asked to match singletrees, blueticks, dashers, walkers, lespedezas, tedders, hame straps, and sweetmilk—if he lived in the country. A city child in Mississippi might be given other tasks.

Culture-specific tests are not new. The $300 million testing industry has simply found marketing such tests for any of the thirty or so small cultural groups unprofitable.

Sixth, if large numbers of children who need assistance are left in the classroom, the regular classroom teacher must be retrained to deal with them in a satisfactory manner. The ideal combination would be a teacher well trained in diagnosis and sequencing in a Piagetian fashion for each classroom, plus a high-impact skills center, with reading and mathematics specialists attached to each primary unit.

A good model for this sort of staffing is the High Challenge program operated by Juanita Jones of the Tulsa, Oklahoma, public schools. This program is funded by USOE. High Challenge teachers use a sophisticated system of short diagnostic tests and teacher observation to work with six or fewer slow children in each classroom. Each teacher is trained to ascertain quickly exactly where the child is in a particular exercise or lesson and to begin a proper sequence of experiences designed to bring him to where he should be. Reading specialists and specialists trained in learning disabilities are attached to each school and are immediately available upon request by a teacher who needs extra assistance in this process.

Another good example of this technique is the group of schools studied by George Weber of the Council for Basic Education. These are schools in depressed areas that are succeeding in spite of great odds. Weber identified critical aspects of these schools as follows:

—A hard-driving no-nonsense administrator who is determined to have a good program

—High expectations for success on the part of every teacher

—Sophisticated use of phonics

—Reading specialists attached to each school

—Sophisticated and heavy use of diagnostic and progress testing

—Progress grouping after the first year with fluid movement between groups [22]

Pressure on school boards and the retraining of very large numbers of teachers will be necessary to accomplish anything. Contrary to popular belief, teachers in depressed areas do not move around a lot. Questions will be raised concerning the fate of special-education teachers if large numbers of children are removed or prevented from being assigned to special-education classes. No danger is eminent. Acccording to figures quoted by USOE officials, only 175,000 special-education teachers are employed. Sixty percent of the retarded children are already in the regular classroom. Special-education teachers would teach many of the new mixed classes under the new system. Many would man the specialist posts and the skill centers. The need for skills of special-education teachers would be greater than ever. The image of both the child and the special-education teacher would change greatly and for the better.

Again, black children can never achieve comparability in achievement or in anything else connected with academic work if an inordinate number are assigned to special-education classes. These classes must be reserved for truly retarded children, and children improperly tested and misplaced must be returned to the regular classrooms. Skill centers manned by special-education personnel must be a part of every school and previously written-off children brought into the academic mainstream.

Notes for Chapter 2

[1] Albert Murray, *South to a Very Old Place* (New York: McGraw-Hill, 1971).

[2] U.S. Census Reports, *Family Income and Characteristics,* Series P-20, No. 204, July, 1970.

[3] Donald Morrison, Editorial in *Phi Delta Kappan* (May, 1972), p. 538.

[4] *Your School's Desegregation—How Real?,* Integrated Education Associates, Chicago, 1972.

[5] Jane Mercer, "Socio-cultural Factors in the Educational Evaluation of Black and Chicano Children" (Paper presented at the Tenth Annual Conference on Civil and Human Rights of Educators and Students, National Education Association, Center for Human Relations, Washington, D.C., February, 1972).

[6] Merle Karnes, *Structured Cognitive Approach for Educating Young Children: Report of a Successful Program* (Technical Bulletin, National Leadership Institute in Teacher Education, University of Connecticut, 1972).

[7] *High-Impact Programs for Disadvantaged Minority Children* (Technical Bulletin, National Leadership Institute in Teacher Education, University of Connecticut, 1972).

[8] *DISTAR Orientation Manual,* Science Research Associates, Chicago, 1971.

[9] Jonathan Kozol, *Death at An Early Age* (Boston: Houghton Mifflin, 1972).

[10] Stephen Strickland, "Can Slum Children Learn?" *American Education* (July, 1971), pp. 3–7.

[11] Waterloo, Iowa, Public Schools, *Home Start* (Information Booklet, 1972).

[12] *Guidelines to Initiate and Operate a Cooperative Vocational Education Program,* Pennsylvania State Department of Education, 1971.

[13] Clifford Stallings, *Gifted Disadvantaged Children* (Technical Bulletin, National Leadership Institute in Teacher Education, University of Connecticut, 1972).

[14] William Labov, "Black Intelligence and Academic Ignorance," *Atlantic* (May 1972), pp. 58–67.

[15] *Public Policy Report: Secondary Vocational Education,* National Association of Manufacturers, 1972.

[16] U.S. Office of Education, *Equality of Educational Opportunity,* 1965.

[17] A. J. Mayeske, "The Coleman Report Re-Visited" (Paper read at the 1971 Conference of the American Psychological Association, Washington, D.C.).

[18] R. D. Russell, "Black Perceptions of Guidance," *Personnel and Guidance Journal* (May, 1970), pp. 721–28.

[19] National Association of Manufacturers, op. cit., p. 10–11.

[20] Lloyd Dunn, "Special Education for the Mildly Retarded: Is Much of it Justifiable?" *Exceptional Children* (1968), pp. 5–22.

[21] Mercer, op. cit., p. 1.

[22] George Weber, *Inner City Children Can Be Taught to Read* (Washington, D.C.; Council for Basic Education, 1971).

CHAPTER 3

Continuing Education

B LACK youth and adults receive an invaluable amount of quality education from adult-education programs, street academies, continuation schools, military schools, manpower training, New Careers, and antipoverty programs.[1] Part-time courses at community colleges, short courses in university extension centers, and television instruction are all potentially good sources of constantly broadening and sharpening the reservoir of black skills and talent. The New Careers education program of the U.S. Office of Education can be a good source of talent development. Apprenticeship programs are finally being opened to blacks. Blacks are also gaining excellent skills in the Black Capitalism program for young businessmen and in cooperatives operated by the black church and other groups.

The unevenness of education in America and the difficulty of delivery of quality education to poor children and youth combine to increase the value of the far-flung continuing-education efforts to the black community. Continuing education is becoming a basic necessity for both whites and blacks in all walks of life. One only has to read Alvin Toffler's *Future Shock* to appreciate this new development in American life. Toffler notes that the American child born today will work at a job not in existence at this time, live in three states, change jobs six times, and retrain himself three times.[2]

Continuing education is vast; estimates show that more people enroll in some form of continuing education than in the public-private schools (fifty million) and higher education (eight million) combined. A relatively silent operation, virtually no public efforts to reform or improve it are apparent. Indeed, student motivation in continuing education is perhaps the most intense there is because of the highly focused and pragmatic nature of the operation. Financial support usually comes from similar pragmatic sources.

An analysis of the participation and potentials of the various programs in continuing education as they relate to black youth and adults follows. Considerations of possible expansions and improvements are made in this context, and new directions based on program experiences and outcomes are identified.

Continuation Schools

Continuation schools are small high schools operated for adolescents who for any reason are unable to continue in the five-day, thirty-six-week high school of the average school system. In a good school system, students are never considered dropouts. They are regarded as having to change their *form* of education from time to time. Education is considered a lifelong process and high school is an interlude of 720 days comprising roughly 3,000 hours of serious instruction plus one-half this amount of hours in home study. This interlude may be completed in contiguous years or it may be completed over a longer period of time. The school system takes the responsibility of offering varied opportunities for students, both adolescents and adults, to complete their studies. The General Education Development diploma is awarded upon successful completion of the GED examination, and the student can move on to higher education or progress in his job.

The GED diploma is one of the success stories of post–World War II education. Nearly 300,000 persons received this diploma in 1971 and the number has been increasing annually. All sorts of continuing-education programs culminate in this diploma. The diploma and testing procedures are described in detail below, but more here on continuation schools and their potential for enabling black youth to change their forms of education and eventually qualify for this certificate.

A good example of an effective continuation school is Reid High of Long Beach, California.[3] California has had continuation schools and community colleges for many years. This advancement is surely a factor in the excellent graduation and college-attendance records of its black students.

Reid enrolls students who must change their forms of education for a variety of reasons. Some have to get work to support themselves or help in family support, some took time off to get married, others moved into the district in the middle of the semester, and still others adjust better to small units like Reid (215 students) than to the large impersonal high schools.

Reid has a faculty of twelve teachers, a counselor, and a part-time vice principal. The enrollment swells somewhat in the spring of the year and an additional teacher is added.

Forty percent of Reid's students work part-time and attend school for only a half day. Reid's program is therefore organized to move the students through the instructional program on a performance basis. Twenty courses are offered and credit is granted on a productive hour system. A total of seventy-five productive class periods of forty-five minutes each constitutes a semester's work for which one-half Carnegie unit (a year of high school work in one subject) is awarded. The school uses the instructional-package approach with these seventy-five hours, and these packages in turn utilize project learning extensively. The overall result is a program involving an effective degree of gestalt-based (where students understand the wholeness of programs) teacher-student planning supported by an insightful system of interim rewards—successful completion of instructional packets, use of semester instead of year-long courses, use of instructional hours and competence level as criteria for course completion.

Reid's classes are small and informal, and latitude is provided through the project method for students to pursue individual interests. The school has a drama club and occasionally publishes a school newspaper. Assemblies are conducted from time to time at the behest of faculty, administrators, or students.

In a study of student response to the Reid program, 90 percent expressed positive feelings with respect to school efforts to personalize instruction. Over 86 percent indicated that they were doing better at Reid than at their previous high school.

Continuation high schools can help many black students who find themselves faced with increasing stress in their efforts to continue in the regular high-school program. If black students in depressed areas are to be served well, continuation high schools are not as widespread or as well-known as they need to be. Every school district with any number of poor black students might well operate a continuation school. The cost is negligible and funds utilized are due the students in any case.

Several school practices might be employed to make continuation schools effective in depressed areas of the black community. Some of these practices are listed below:

1. The term *school dropout* might be eliminated from school lexicon.
2. Education as a lifelong process might be stressed by both word and deed by all hands.
3. A larger number of poor black students should be *expected* to have to change their *form* of education because of the stresses and strains of poverty and bigotry.
4. Changes in *forms* of education—not dropping out— should be the description applied to these students.
5. Continuation schools should be assured of a good—even a heroic—image.
6. The schools should be well advertised in schools and communities as viable alternatives to situations that may be less than desirable.
7. Use of instructional packets, criterion testing, and GED certificates or diplomas might enable schools to place the entire program on a performance basis. Completion of a certain number of hours of instruction and Carnegie units could then be eliminated.
8. Concerted efforts to involve community groups would result in a tremendous amount of support and encouragement for students to continue their schooling.
9. Students who have left school and have yet to become

engaged in another form of education might be recruited by continuation-school counselors to elect the continuation school as their form of lifelong education for this juncture in their lives.

10. Sports and other curriculum activities at regular high schools might involve continuation-school students as regular members of their units.

11. The machinery of obtaining GED diplomas might well be part of the ongoing information services in the regular high schools of poor black youth. Most black youth are not aware that the GED exists.

12. Success stories of recipients of GED diplomas might well be part of this information service. Return of alumni who have gone on to good jobs or to college is a tried and true method of providing role models for black youth driven to the wall by grinding poverty and bigotry.

Again, creative and matter-of-fact expansion of continuation schools seems a viable means of enabling most black youth and young adults to obtain the schooling and certification they will need in the coming years. Part of the agenda for the black community might well be working to get these schools in every community.

General Education Development Certificate

The General Education Development Certificate is known by various names. High-school equivalency diploma, GED certificate, and HEP (high-school equivalency program) are all used to describe what has become one of the success stories of modern education.

The GED Testing Program (the official name) is sponsored by the Commission on Accreditation of Service Experiences, a unit of the American Council on Education. The commission was established in 1945 to evaluate achievements of military personnel in a variety of situations. Since 1945, the commission has worked with state departments of education in all states, departments of education in American Samoa, the Canal Zone, Guam, Puerto Rico, and the Trust Territory of the Pacific Islands, along with the departments of education of the Canadian Provinces of Nova Scotia and Saskatchewan. The diplomas or certificates are widely accepted in lieu of high-school diplomas. Business, industry, civil-service commissions, and state and local boards of licensing examiners all recognize them as meeting the requirements of high-school graduation for job eligibility and promotion. Many colleges and universities admit students on the basis of this diploma. Some of the most effective college students have been veterans who have entered college via GED certificates. Similarly, the armed forces accept GED diplomas in lieu of a high-school diploma and use these diplomas for assignment to service schools and for promotion in billets.[3] A total of 387,733 persons took the GED test in 1971 and 231,558 certificates were issued on the basis of this testing. This figure is almost a tenfold increase from the 39,016 who took the test in 1949. The GED potential for assisting black youth and adults is unmatched anywhere.

Most examinees take the GED test at official GED centers. Currently, 1,858 centers for this service are available.[4] Centers are located in accredited high schools or colleges, at adult schools, boards of education, community colleges, and at state departments of education. Each state department of education develops its own policies regarding location of centers, level of test competence, minimum age of examinee, and cooperates with the commission on security of the test, general policies for issuance of certificates, criteria for admission to GED testing, and other uses of test results.

The GED test is an excellent measure of educational attainment, for the results are often more valid than many high-school diplomas. Five comprehensive examinations comprise the GED:

1. English
2. Social Studies
3. Natural Sciences
4. Literature
5. Mathematics

GED test policies vary from state to state. The commission recommends a minimum age of nineteen for admission to the test to avoid placing the program in direct competition with ongoing programs of secondary education. The commission recommends also that anyone residing in state be considered eligible for testing. Level of test competence is left to the states. Even though variations exist, a standard score of 35 on each of five tests and a standard score of 45 on all five tests is a common criterion for awarding the diploma. These scores represent about the twentieth percentile for all high-school seniors in the nation and such a policy is quite selective in nature.

The GED test is also widely utilized by the military and is administered through the U.S. Armed Forces Institute. Both the Veterans Administration in its hospitals and federal and state agencies in their correctional institutions use the GED test to certify those individuals who are taking high-school completion courses. Tests are available for handicapped students and Spanish versions are available.

For the 37 percent of young adult blacks who failed to change their form of education last year, the GED program represents an outstanding method of obtaining a direly needed certification in a very short period of time through a variety of routes. In a perfect world, 185,000 black youth would divide themselves among quality continuation schools, street academies, Job Corps centers, adult-education programs, military classes, manpower programs, and antipoverty operations. A year or so of hard part-time study later, they would present themselves for examination at their nearest GED center. The GED program can become the second-chance school system of the black community. High on the agenda for the black community would be creative efforts to have young people fully utilize this vital ladder out of poverty. By developing creative programs and policies designed for young blacks, state departments of education and the GED commission could take a giant step toward assisting these young people. Some suggestions follow:

1. The policy of requiring young people to wait until their

nineteenth birthday to apply for GED diplomas might be changed to allow seventeen-year-olds to make application. This policy would encourage youngsters at age sixteen, the official school-leaving age, to enroll directly in continuation schools and other forms of continuing education. Most students would take the examination at eighteen, but the carrot of being able to do so at seventeen or as soon thereafter as possible is a powerful motivator. A policy of nineteen years of age as minimum requirement for testing places a three-year moratorium on schooling as far as the sixteen-year-old is concerned. Discouragement sets in, interest flags, and the job of re-involvement in schooling becomes doubly difficult.

2. Information campaigns in the black community on the diploma, its value, and the myriad ways to obtain it might step up black participation considerably.

3. Advisory panels of blacks in each of the eighteen hundred or so communities where GED centers are located would be mutually beneficial in carrying the word and avoiding mistakes.

4. Antipoverty agencies would pick up the tab in many communities for GED testing (about $5) for poor youth and adults. Community agencies everywhere might do this.

5. A variety of independent-study approaches to preparation for the tests might be encouraged. Peer tutoring, programmed study, and correspondence courses might all be utilized to enable large numbers of youth who cannot or will not enroll in formal continuing education to take personal responsibility and initiative for their own education.

6. The social studies, literature, and English portions of the tests might incorporate more material from black culture and black studies to increase their relevancy for black youth.

7. Efforts might be made to emphasize the quality of the examination. It is easier to serve time in high school and graduate, for example, than to pass an examination placing one at the twentieth to twenty-fifth percentile of all graduating seniors.

Military Schools

Some of the best education blacks have received over the years has come from the vast military education operation. Options for the 185,000 black adolescents who reach the age of seventeen without continuing their education must surely include this viable form of schooling.

Military schools are diverse in their operations. In a time of need, the military will take a completely illiterate draftee or enlistee and teach him to read and write in a short period of time. At the other end of the spectrum, a gifted young black may be sent to medical school in return for a number of years of service in its medical corps. In between is a vast array of adult education, service schools, and special college attendance operations.

Most of the preparatory school and college study is directed by the United States Armed Forces Institute located at Madison, Wisconsin. USAFI contracts with the University of Wisconsin for a variety of its operations and runs others with its own personnel.

USAFI offers over two hundred courses in elementary, high school, college, and technical subjects in regular classroom and independent-study situations. These courses are offered at military installations around the world. In addition, five thousand correspondence courses at the baccalaureate and graduate levels are made available through USAFI contracts with extension divisions of forty-four accredited colleges and universities.[5] The military also operates technical courses and training programs totaling in the thousands for its own benefit.

A black candidate for continuing education has available to him high-school courses in English, literature, mathematics, social studies, science, business administration, and classical and foreign languages. College courses are available in these same areas. Technical courses are available at both high-school and college levels. They include aviation studies, auto mechanics, building construction, electricity, electronics, diesel engines, metalworking, radio and television, and refrigeration.

Project 100,000, an adult-education program for recruits

who fail to meet test score standards for enlistment in the military, has proved successful. Under normal circumstances, military enlistments or drafts are limited to men who score at levels I, II, and III on a five-level scale of the Armed Forces Qualification Test, the basic test in the armed forces. Such a policy insures induction of men with academic skills at or above entering high-school level. These men—and this is important— are thus able to enroll in the basic GED program and pursue high-school work on a continuing basis during their military tours. Elementary school education is not usually offered in years of peace when a large army is not necessary.

When the antipoverty campaign shifted into high gear in the mid-sixties, the Defense Department unveiled a new program to enlist or draft men in level IV and in some cases level V and to enroll these men in intensive all-day basic education de- signed to raise them to at least level III and perhaps above. The men were also given intensive medical treatment and if necessary were recycled in their basic training program of military skills.

The men were not labeled as special recruits or draftees and only the company commander was aware of their special needs. Most importantly, all instruction utilized the most advanced methods, materials, and media in the world. The results were astonishing. For each three weeks of instruction, the men gained one year on standardized tests. Instruction was sched- uled five days a week for eight hours per day giving each man a total of 120 hours of instruction—comparing favorably with the amount of time spent on a subject in a school year.

Blacks receive a goodly amount of excellent education from military schools. Annually, blacks comprise roughly 400,000 of the three-million-man military establishment. Traditionally, poor Southern blacks, like poor Southern whites, have utilized the military as a career resource. Others have used the armed forces as a career ladder; as a place to get a job, gain skills, save money, and accumulate benefits such as the G.I. Bill. The sixteen black generals and one black admiral in the mili- tary of the 1970s are shining examples to young blacks of the rewards of hard work, hard study, and perseverance.

Fuller utilization of military schooling will contribute to the quality education drive immeasurably. Some suggestions follow:

1. High-school students might be better apprised of opportunities and advantages of military schooling by increased emphasis on this schooling as a viable form of continuing education.

2. The military might interest a larger number of black students in its educational programs by increased utilization of black colleges for its extension courses. Many military bases are located in the South near black colleges. Race relations being what they are, black soldiers would more readily sign up for a course offered by Jackson State than the University of Mississippi.

3. Programs such as Project 100,000 might be continued regardless of whether the country is at war or peace or whether an intensified antipoverty drive is in progress or not. It is a good, basic form of adult education and helps whites as well as blacks.

4. More black colleges might be utilized as GED testing centers. This assertion would increase the knowledge and appreciation of the program in the black community and result in greater participation.

5. All branches of the armed forces might develop preparatory programs similar to the U.S. Navy's BOOST schools described earlier. This type of preparation will swell enrollments in the academies and the spillover will be directed into other colleges and universities.

Apprenticeship Programs

Apprenticeship programs have not been a source of schooling for blacks because of a long history of bigotry and discrimination. Sadly, this country boasted a higher percentage of black skilled craftsmen during the slavery years than in 1950. With the coming of the labor unions in the 1930s, black craftsmen were pushed out of the trades and their skills often died with them as closed-shop unions barred their sons from apprentice-ship programs.

Considerable progress has been made in forcing unions to admit black apprentices, but much more pressure is needed. As of July, 1972, the number of black apprentices totaled 12,550. This number represented 6.7 percent of the 186,236 apprentices registered and a 91 percent increase over the 6,561 blacks registered four years earlier. In a more improved situation at least, 20,000 black apprentices would be enrolled.[6]

The big generator in this drive is the affirmative action programs of the Department of Labor, which oversees apprenticeship programs. The widely publicized battles to break down discrimination in the construction trades also seem to be bearing fruit. One-half of all apprentices are enrolled in these trades, and 7,983 of 110,592 were black (7.2 percent). Black metal manufacturing apprentices totaled 5.1 percent, mining 4.9 percent, utilities and transportation 8 percent, and trades and services 7.5 percent. The intensity of this drive might be gauged by noting that black apprenticeships rose although total apprenticeships decreased. Figure 13 contains data in this re-

FIGURE 13
BLACK APPRENTICE ENROLLMENT 1968–1972

	Date	Total	Blacks	Percent
All Trades	12–31–68	166,087	6,561	4.0
	12–31–69	201,574	9,331	4.6
	12–31–70	199,928	11,045	5.5
	12–31–71	186,236	12,550	6.7
Building and	12–31–68	91,177	3,728	4.0
Construction	12–31–69	107,592	5,193	4.8
Trades	12–31–70	112,890	6,732	6.0
	12–31–71	110,592	7,983	7.2

SOURCE: *Black News Digest*, U.S. Department of Labor, July 24, 1972.

spect. Black apprentices are often subjected to intensive racism once enrolled in the program, and wise communities would make every effort to ease this impact in every possible way available to them. A good start has been made by the Labor Department with the appointment of blacks to key regional posts in its Bureau of Apprenticeship and Training. Regional directors coupled with regional directors of Equal Employment Opportunity Commission programs can do much to monitor affirmative action programs in this respect.

Black apprenticeship participation might also be improved by the following strategies:

1. Better career education might be stressed to acquaint children with the advantages of apprenticeships and the rewards of being a skilled craftsman.
2. More pressure might be placed on Southern unions for obvious reasons.
3. More technical-school programs offering apprenticeship credit might be developed in the black community. Many crafts award two years of apprenticeship credit for graduation from a good technical-school curriculum.
4. Black craftsmen must be assured regular work when the journeyman's card is won. Some of the highly touted government plans in this area have been less than fully effective. A *New York Times,* editorial of July 30, 1972, reports, for example, that after three years of talk and several hundred thousand dollars of funding, the New York Plan for Affirmative Action had resulted in only twenty-two additional black journeymen in the construction trades. *The Times* went on to say that this money and publicity had not been expended entirely for naught. The director of the program had been called to Washington to become a special assistant to the President for labor affairs.
5. The apprenticeship program per se might be expanded. Because of a shortage of craftsmen, the prices for their services are sky-high. But, like the American Medical Association, the unions keep the number of practitioners small by controlling training slots.

Paraprofessional Programs

The antipoverty program has initiated the successful paraprofessional programs emerging from the Office of Economic Opportunity and operated by various agencies of the government. Over 500,000 paraprofessionals have been trained and employed in American school systems. An estimated 100,000 have been developed for the health professions and untold numbers for other areas of work. Blacks participate heavily in these programs. The better programs offer extensive training and career ladders and offer blacks a fine opportunity literally to work and learn their way up the ladder.[7]

Paraprofessionals enter their work and learning at various stages of development. Some have less than a high-school education and are given the opportunity to pursue part-time study toward the GED diploma. In one of the more successful programs, the Career Opportunity Program of the U.S. Office of Education, ten thousand paraprofessionals are pursuing work toward the bachelor's degree at colleges and universities.

Paraprofessionals perform a variety of tasks in schools and other agencies. The school program of Minneapolis is a good example of a paraprofessional program in action. Minneapolis refers to these workers as auxiliary personnel. A six-step career ladder for three categories of workers is provided. The basic entry level is School Aide I with a beginning salary of $3,030 per year rising to $4,333 in step six. School Aide II salaries range from $3,485 to $4,622 a year and School Assistants start at $5,151 and end at $6,666. Advancement beyond a minimum level requires a stipulated minimum of approved training in all categories.

Auxiliary personnel in Minneapolis schools perform a variety of functions. They help with classroom routines, serve as school-community liaison, tutor, develop materials, and in the case of school assistants, take over classes in the limited absence of the regular teacher.

School Aide I applicants must pass a civil-service examination to be employed. School Aide II must have a high-school diploma or a GED certificate, must have completed forty-five quarter credits in training, and must be still enrolled in a training program. School assistants must have completed sixty quarter credits of training, must be enrolled in training, and must have served as School Aide II for one year. The career ladder aspects of the program are clear and the motivational advantages are enormous.

Jane Smith, age twenty and four years out of school (having left school at the end of the tenth grade), might very well find a way of continuing her education at her local hospital, school board, or city manager's office through a paraprofessional program. All of the ingredients for success are present. She can perform badly needed work for agencies serving the public. She can continue to support herself while continuing her education, and she can move up a career ladder as far as her drive and connections will carry her.

The University of Minnesota graduated about one dozen paraprofessionals from its Career Opportunity programs in June of 1972. Many of these young people are now pursuing graduate studies. A great possibility for success in a few years are the Ph.D. and M.D. recipients who began their studies as paraprofessionals. Black people make these sorts of advances.

Hospitals, parks, schools, public-safety units, and the new ecology legions are strapped for personnel. Young blacks are searching desperately for job entry and for a way to continue their schooling. A national target of five million federally funded paraprofessional slots would enable large numbers of poor blacks to combine work and learning at a relatively moderate cost and would enable state and local agencies to serve people better. Two million paraprofessionals could be easily utilized just to clean up our ten largest cities.

Paraprofessional programs are usually well planned and administered. However, some can serve black communities better. Some strategies for achieving this goal follow:

1. The government should expand the program as outlined above.

2. All programs might be required to offer career ladder opportunities.

3. Huge amounts of money might be pumped into programs in the South. The need is great and little exists to assist black youth and offer them an alternative to migration to large cities. The Georgia high-school graduation rate, for example, is only 44 percent. This low rate places a strain on Atlanta and Chicago as more of these undereducated youngsters become undereducated young adults and migrate.

4. Southern (and some Northern) programs must specify full black participation and receive careful monitoring to assure this.

5. Every professional association might be encouraged to develop paraprofessional programs.

6. Information programs in schools might stress the value of paraprofessional programs together with information on involvement for interested students.

7. Service industries, such as hotel management and transportation, might be encouraged to develop paraprofessional programs.

Again, the paraprofessional movement offers an excellent means for poor black youth to work and study their way into meaningful occupations in areas that might make excellent use of their talents. The key to full use of this valuable avenue to a better economic position is expansion of paraprofessional programs through federal funding. Ideally, every talented black youngster unable to continue his education through formal channels would be able to do so through paraprofessional programs.

One of the most important outcomes is the close contact with professional work and life. Black workers who partially climb the career ladder of a paraprofessional program can almost always be counted on to set higher goals and aspirations for their children. Important, too, the participants have gained valuable insights regarding operations of professional workers and the routes and short cuts their children can use to become one.

Government expenditures in the paraprofessional area pay dividends far beyond reasonable expectations.

The Job Corps

The Job Corps has had a successful, albeit a stormy, history. Since 1965, the federal government has offered a combination of educational and vocational training to 325,000 disadvantaged youths, more than 75 percent of whom have been black. These young people were perhaps the most brutalized in American society. More than 85 percent had never seen a dentist or physician. Nearly this many were malnourished and most had fallen behind in their school work. Almost none were in school at the time and few were working.[8]

The Job Corps took these youngsters into residential centers where complete medical checkups were given and a steady diet of nourishing foods provided. In addition to room, board, and clothing, Job Corps provided a small stipend for spending money each month. One of the best educational programs in the country was provided, and after a certain level of competence was reached, corpsmen moved into a sophisticated technical-training program. After graduation, assistance was provided in finding a job and becoming established in the position. Many of these Job Corps graduates joined the army. Some went to college or into paraprofessional programs.

The Job Corps is now operated by the Department of Labor. Ideally, about 25,000 students are enrolled at any given time. The average stay at a center is about five months, although one could possibly spend two years in the Job Corps. The program is popular with older congressmen because of its similarity to the old Civilian Conservation Corps, which many attended during the Depression years. In a Labor Department news release dated May 21, 1973, Assistant Secretary of Labor William Kolberg announced that the Job Corps would be "somewhat smaller in numbers but will be, I believe, a much more effective program in preparing severely disadvantaged youth for the world of work." Kolberg was addressing the annual national conference of Women in Community Service (WICS), a mainstay in the recruitment activities of the Job Corps. He noted that the program would be regionalized and that labor unions and business would be involved to a much greater extent.

A variety of corporations and organizations operate Job Corps centers. In Jersey City, New Jersey, for example, the program is operated by the Young Women's Christian Association. This group operates a 750-bed facility that in 1972 trained nearly 1,500 young women in cosmetology, electronic assembly, business and clerical jobs, and allied health occupations. The Philco-Ford Corporation in Guthrie, Oklahoma, trained about 1,900 young women in the same areas plus drafting and lithography.

Job Corps operations include thirty-two conservation centers located in national parks or forests, thirty-eight urban or nearby urban centers, and two Puerto Rican centers. The Corps maintains three mini-centers for highly disadvantaged youths. The mini-centers are limited to thirty beds each, provide special counseling and tutorial programs, and utilize high schools and technical-training programs in the communities they serve.

Almost all Job Corps enrollees take the GED test and the success rate is high. The instructional program of the centers is excellent. Upon arrival at the center, a youth is administered several short-form placement tests in various areas. He is then assigned a work carrel and a set of programmed materials and assigned to work a little below his level of operating competence. Upon completion of these units of work, the enrollee is administered a series of short criterion-referenced tests to ascertain level of mastery and given more units to work on. If he hits a snag, a course tutor works with him on an individual basis until he is ready to move on his own again. In addition to his carrel and programmed books, the youngster has available to him a wide variety of audio tapes, video cassettes, eight-millimeter single-concept film loops, and a library. Discussion groups periodically allow for verbalization of his new learnings and unit tests keep him moving.

The big reward for quick completion of the educational program is the opportunity to take a crack at the GED diploma examination and/or the movement into full-time study of a technical occupation. The beauty of the Job Corps program is the provision for plug-ins of students at any point in the program, the provision for steady self-paced learning, and the provision for an immediate payoff for hard concentrated work. Job Corpsmen do not have to wait either for a new semester to start in order to start learning or for a teacher to get himself and twenty-five students ready to teach. The quicker he masters the curriculum, the quicker he is able to begin and finish his technical training, get a job, and begin to make money.

The Job Corps has helped many poor black youth and promises to help many more. If 35,000 of the annual 50,000 served are black, and if the program is continued for the next thirty years, a viable unit for dealing with the most mangled segment of out-of-school and out-of-work black youth will be available.

Some of the best educational minds in the country worked on developing the Job Corps. Some suggestions for improvements follow:

1. Job Corps centers might well be doubled and a goal of serving 100,000 Corpsmen a year might well be set. The biggest complaint about the Job Corps in the black community is that the youngsters can't get into the program because of a lack of slots.

2. More Job Corps centers might be set up in rural areas. Some parents would agree to sending a seventeen-year-old to a national forest camp who demur at sending the youngster to Jersey City because of the fast pace of the city.

   A problem exists with political pressure of people in towns near national preserves who want a federal installation nearby but shiver at the thought of a few free-wheeling blacks on the town streets. A Job Corps camp for Yorktown, Virginia, was first planned and then abandoned because of this concern. The federal government, in reality, was unable to exercise an option on federal lands because of this pressure. This sort of thing should not be allowed to happen.

3. More black groups might be given operating contracts for Job Corps centers. Some of the new black entrepreneurs might join some of the black civic and fraternal groups now operating centers.

4. Successful Job Corps graduates might be utilized as information specialists in junior high schools in black communities. The intent is to make youngsters aware of options available to them for further education.

5. Work experience programs might be utilized in centers near industrial complexes. The intent is to move Job Corpsmen into work regimens while still offering the supportive situations of the Job Corps center.

6. Job Corps stipends might be raised as cost of living goes up.

7. The Job Corps utilizes the Computer Job Bank of the U.S. Employment Service. This service enables job applicants in twelve hundred or so communities to apply for job openings anywhere in a state by utilizing daily computer print-outs from each office regarding available jobs. Job Corps centers in communities without this service might make it available to young people on a daily basis.

The JOBS Program

After the riots of the mid-sixties, President Lyndon B. Johnson rallied the business community to provide the one element that makes an immediate difference in the lives of poor black adults—jobs. Admittedly a choke program designed literally to quench the urban flames, the Jobs in the Business Sector (JOBS) program has been a success. The parent body of JOBS is the National Alliance of Businessmen (NAB). NAB is a powerful group of corporate executives. More than twenty thousand corporations and businesses have worked with the program through 180 metropolitan offices. All executives of the organizations are on loan from corporations.

NAB works closely with the Labor Department, utilizing government funds for recruiting and training workers, for awareness training of staff and other workers, and for placement. Nearly 800,000 workers have been employed and trained through this program. A pilot program of tax credits for hiring severely deprived individuals has been initiated in two cities. In four summers since 1968, nearly 600,000 young people have been hired for summer jobs.[9]

This program is a fine example of part equal opportunity and part concern for the poor, both emanating from self-interest on the part of the business community. Ironically, riots and violence were required to force American business to share opportunities with black Americans. A closer look is needed to see how underutilized black talent can gain job entry through this medium, consolidate their gains, and succeed.

In this respect, the JOBS upgrading program is of particular significance. Working with the Department of Labor, JOBS has re-examined program marketing techniques, employee eligibility, skill training components, support services, and training costs. The purpose is to develop a practical program of career ladders instead of dead-end jobs for entry-level JOBS workers. Expansion of this program to include all black workers would eliminate a thorny problem in equal opportunity programs: vertical movement of entry-level black personnel.

The NAB has an excellent working relationship with black colleges. Presently working through a network of 39 cluster groups of corporations and black colleges, plans call for 128 clusters involving all black colleges together with the 20,000 corporations participating in NAB.

The NAB also operates a Youth Motivation Task Force, which has great potential. The impact of bigotry can be so devastating on black youth that many simply do not believe that meaningful job openings will ever be available to them, and the only meaningful thing they can accomplish is to pick up the gun. The Youth Motivation Task Force tried to overcome this problem by putting living witnesses from NAB corporations into the community, classroom, and clubs. The YMTF operated in twenty-five metropolitan areas in 1970–71. Three thousand successful businessmen and women who talked to more than 25,000 poor black youth were involved.[10]

The NAB is incorporated in the District of Columbia as a nonprofit national corporation with a $6 million budget provided by cash contributions and the Department of Labor. A significant addition to operating expenses is the loan of executive talent to the corporation. More than three thousand workers were working on NAB projects and receiving salaries from corporations.

The NAB is a viable aid in providing the missing link in the drive of black Americans for equal opportunity. President Nixon stated the case bluntly in his inaugural address when he promised to do everything possible to "cut blacks in and assure them a piece of the action." Said differently, white corporations must be led to see that for continued peace and economic vibrancy, they cannot (with government assistance) corner the market on the production and distribution of goods and services in America, control seven of eight jobs in the economy, and deny 12 percent of the population full participation in this most important aspect of life: the means to earn a living. The continuance of this policy simply will not work.

The NAB is a method of educating businessmen to these facts of life through direct participation in problems generated by misguided efforts of business and government to deny economic participation of blacks. The association's program is also a method of offering a dynamic form of job training and skills to both disadvantaged and better-off blacks. The effort should be applauded, expanded, and improved. Some strategies for accomplishing these things follow:

1. The expansion of NAB as described above might become a reality. Every major and minor metropolitan area with concentrations of blacks might have a JOBS program.
2. The cluster approach used with black colleges might be extended to a comparable number of large black high schools.

3. JOBS programs might utilize the U.S. Employment Service computer print-outs to reach into rural areas of the Deep South where many blacks still live in poverty and isolation.
4. The JOBS career-ladder programs might observe the paraprofessional programs in action and borrow from their experience and storehouse of knowledge.
5. The JOBS Youth Motivation Task Force program might attempt to penetrate remote areas of the Deep South. There are levers to be used in dealing with bigotry in these areas. Corporate power and branch plants and distribution facilities can and, in some cases, are opening up jobs to blacks in these areas. "Living successes" from these efforts might be pressed into service to generate more attempts on the part of black youth to penetrate the system.
6. Continued innovative thinking by the Labor Department is essential in these efforts.

Manpower Training Programs

Manpower training programs are perhaps the largest, most expensive and one of the more effective methods of continuing education. More than a million persons enroll in a wide variety of programs each year. All receive technical training and are supported by stipends while training. Some participants receive basic adult education to increase academic skills plus technical education.

Manpower training programs were developed by the Department of Labor in response to a perceived need to make adjustments for a labor force experiencing dislocations caused by automation of production processes and geographical shifts in both population and production centers. The first programs began in 1962 and were patterned on the manpower operations of Sweden, which retrains about 2 percent of its work force annually with government support. The U.S. government now spends about a billion dollars a year on manpower training.

One possibly may receive manpower training in almost any skill in the trade, industrial, service, and clerical areas through this program. Institutional programs offer 1,000 to 1,500 hours of training in a variety of occupations and on-the-job training programs, which pay part of the costs of training to employers for worker-trainees in the hope that a permanent slot will be provided for the trainee upon graduation. A worker-mobility project finds a job for a trainee in another locality and pays moving costs to the job site and renders supportive services to the worker upon arrival.

Manpower programs are varied. Proprietary schools are pressed into service on occasion. Proprietary schools are operated for profit, such as the data-processing institutes. The Urban League prepares prospective apprentice trainees for entrance exams through the program.

One of the most innovative programs is a college preparatory program for dropouts in New York City. The manpower program has placed more than 517 black and Puerto Rican youngsters in the city's community colleges in the last three years. Eighty percent remain in college, a very high retention rate compared to the usual college experience.[11] Called the College Adapter Program (CAP), this operation recruits, tests, and screens dropouts with at least a seventh-grade reading skill and high motivation to attend college. Neighborhood Youth Corps counselors, manpower recruiters, friends, and relatives join in this hunt. The recruits receive a two-week orientation program and a twenty-week instructional program in mathematics, science, language, and electives. This schedule is supplemented by tutoring, frequent testing, and homework. Most students work for one-half day. Supportive services such as child care and housing are provided when needed, and a manpower stipend of $30 to $45 a week to cover transportation, books, and incidentals is provided. All graduates are placed and continue to receive stipends and tutoring at community colleges. In short, the manpower program of New York is operating one of the most effective preparatory schools in the country and utilizing college for what it has really become to many young people in America: a manpower training center.

Manpower programs have problems. Some train for dead-end jobs; others have trouble placing their graduates because of bigotry and discrimination. Some blacks have been graduated from as many as three retraining programs. On the whole, the project is imparting skills and updating skills of blacks and having a ripple effect in black communities. Hopefully, the program will be expanded. In an ideal situation, about two million Americans would be retrained annually at a cost of $3 billion and blacks would comprise half this number.

Some strategies that might enable manpower programs to expand effectively are listed here:

1. Labor mobility thrusts might be stressed. Fifty percent of the black population moved to the city in the past twenty years, changing blacks from rural to metropolitan (78 percent) dwellers. Black workers had to make this trip alone in most cases, find an unskilled job, set up house in a slum, and send for their families when bus fare was finally accumulated. Sometimes the search for work was futile and the insults brutal. "We don't pick cotton at Kodak" was the curt reply to Minister Florence's plea for jobs for his congregation by the president of the Kodak Corporation. Shortly, Rochester began to burn. Blacks are still moving from small towns and Southern farms into big metropolitan areas. They should arrive at the gates to the city armed with new skills learned in down-home manpower centers, with housing allowances and hiring papers in hand. They should be met by manpower mobility people and helped to settle into their new life.

2. The college preparatory programs might be expanded. Colleges are in reality new forms of manpower centers, and manpower programs can be used to good advantage to prepare them for participation in these centers.

3. Manpower programs for career advancement might be developed to enable workers to learn skills part-time and move up in their jobs.

4. Manpower concepts might effectively be applied to retraining black teachers, social scientists, and others to fill shortages in law and medicine. Many young twenty-four-to-thirty-year-old blacks would leave these professions and

complete medical and legal training if sufficient stipends and training costs could be provided.

5. Pressure and rewards must be used to make employers more acceptable to hiring manpower trainees.
6. Extensive information programs on manpower training might become a part of the high-school curriculum.

Street Academies and Student Schools

In 1966, the Urban League began a program called Street Academies, designed to make contact with alienated youth who had left school and who were not continuing their education in a systematic way. Recruiters were employed who could relate to these youths, and small classes of ten or twelve students were set up in leased stores in the neighborhood. The program has been highly successful. Nearly 24,000 young people have been served, and the concept has been copied widely in regular high schools and in other street efforts.

One group of youngsters in upper New York State set up a student school, a high school of their own. The two hundred or so students can boast of several alumni who have gone on to college and many who have completed the GED diploma requirements and secured good jobs. Students schools hold great promise for enabling alienated youth who are unable to communicate with adults in any meaningful fashion to gain insights into the educational process and develop their talents in their own way. Youngsters make plenty of mistakes in organizing these schools, but for many metropolitan dwellers the alternatives are a student school or no school at all.

An interesting spin-off of street academies has been the postal academies, formerly operated by the Post Office Department and shifted to the Labor Department after reorganization of the Post Office as a corporation. Postal academies operate in six big cities and enroll about fifteen hundred young people in any year. The thrust of postal academies is preparation of youngsters for jobs in the Post Office, in government, industry, and for college entry.

The counseling aspects of street academies and similar units are probably as important as the academic work. In the Sturm und Drang of adolescence, young people are bound to lose their way from time to time. Street academies and student schools enable them to find direction. These relaxed educational forms are viable methods of changing the form of a student's education.

In the Urban League program many youngsters go on to transitional academies, which are more formal schools designed to prepare for GED diplomas. Some of the more able students are sent to Harlem Prep and then to college. The college record of retention for Harlem Prep students, as noted previously, is 100 per cent. Other young people are sent to Newark Prep and still others are enrolled in the ABC (A Better Chance) program, a veteran feeder program that moves black youth into private preparatory schools. In other programs, students sometimes go back to their old high schools.

Street academies and student schools might be considered permanent or semipermanent adjuncts to schools in many cities or substitutes for bad situations. Sadly, some depressed areas in big cities for all intents and purposes do not have a school system. Instead there exist a payroll, a cadre of contemptuous teachers and administrators—chained to black students because they can find no other slots—and school buildings in ruins. Unions and political maneuvering keep the enterprise going but little is accomplished. Some dedicated teachers break their hearts trying to make bricks without straw, the students are mangled, and everybody else pays off the mortgage from the enterprise. Black students in these situations attend school as little as possible out of self-defense and to lessen their exploitation by lowering the state payments for average daily membership. They leave school as soon as possible. These schools in a better world would be bulldozed—the students scattered to other schools or placed in street academies and student schools. When the bulldozers and the faculty had left, a new school might be built and a dedicated professional staff assigned for a fresh start.

In addition to this suggested strategy, street academies and student schools might be made more effective through the following:

1. Street academies might be brought into the NAB-JOBS network in some fashion. Use of the Youth Motivation Task Force might be valuable, as would be the contacts for employment and further study.
2. Student schools might receive support through a modified voucher system. Students would be eligible for a $1,000 voucher to buy education from a student school so long as criterion-referenced tests showed they were making steady progress toward the GED diploma.
3. The preparatory school network described earlier might recruit heavily in street academies and student schools.

The postal academies might be developed in all large cities and perhaps a hundred small towns. The Deep South is yet untouched by this movement and a "straight" organization like the Post Office might be the entrée needed.

Cooperative Programs

Some of the most unusual and promising continuing education is in process in cooperatives. Blacks are expanding their skills in a variety of areas and gaining new insights in an informal manner that almost defies description. Three types of organization seem to generate highly successful cooperatives: the black church, the Office of Economic Opportunity, and Northern missionary-type groups operating in rural areas of the South.

The black church has always been a remarkable phenomenon in getting things done in the black community. When Richard Allen led black Methodists out of the balconies to which they were assigned in the Methodist church in 1793, the first broadly organized black community movement began. Allen set up the African Methodist Episcopal church to the consternation of his fellow Philadelphia Methodists who could not understand why blacks were not grateful for their opportunity to be integrated into the balconies of white churches. The AMEs went on to establish Wilberforce University in Wilberforce, Ohio, before slavery was abolished and a network of black colleges in the South after the Civil War. Working with other black colleges, the AMEs put thirty thousand black teachers into black communities in fifteen years and virtually wiped out black illiteracy in a generation. The AMEs still operate colleges and preparatory schools, build housing projects, import African students to America for schooling, and send AME missionaries to Africa. An AME bishop, Stephen Gill Spottswood, has served as chairman of the board of the NAACP.

Black Baptists are also active in the black community and one of the successes of the antipoverty drives has been the development of the Opportunities Industrialization Corporation by the Reverend Leon Sullivan, a Philadelphia minister. Sullivan developed OIC by raising operating funds in his church and setting up a technical school for unemployed adults in an abandoned jail. He secured loans of machinery and equipment by heavy persuasion from local business and industry. Sullivan told these industrialists that they were saving Pennsylvania money by preventing riots and additions to the relief rolls through loans of their machinery and sometimes technicians to serve as teachers. After a Sullivan pitch, the usual murmur in the executive suite would be "Oh, I see"—hence the name of the group OIC.

In 1972, OICs operated in ninety-eight communities. They stress efficiency and pay no training stipends, thereby insuring that only highly motivated people come to them. They advertise the expertise of their graduates via television and other media and have placed nearly seventy thousand trained people in jobs in the past five years. Sullivan joined the board of directors of General Motors with public pronouncements that his stated aim was the generation of more black GM dealerships, more black subcontracts for parts and components, and more black jobs. All of these objectives are being realized.

Some local black church operations are extraordinary. A case in point is the daring of the Free For All Baptist Church of Atlanta under the leadership of the Reverend W. J. Stafford.

Free For All is just that. Anyone is welcome and no dues and collections are taken. The church is maintained by its cooperative enterprises.

Free For All operates four kindergartens, an apartment complex, and a nightclub in Underground Atlanta, a historical and restored section of the city. The church took a $100,000 option on the Top O' Peachtree restaurant and lounge atop the National Bank of Georgia building. Free For All provides 280 jobs for members ranging from teachers and psychiatrists to drivers of the Free For All buses. Its nightclub band is required to play on Sunday evenings for youth functions at the church.

A good example of missionary-type cooperatives operating with government funds is Penn Community Services of Beaufort County, South Carolina. Penn Services was founded in 1862 at the height of the Civil War. Penn Services' first directors, Laura Toron and Ellen Murray, were Vassar graduates from Philadelphia determined to teach freed slaves how to operate the plantations vacated by their masters. Over the years Penn Services has operated schools, health services, and skills-training programs. In 1969, the organization entered the antipoverty drive with a bang. A marketing cooperative has been formed that tripled the prices farmers and fishermen received for their products. A building cooperative has brought new and bigger building contracts to black firms and a building supply company cuts costs and makes jobs. A nonstock, nonprofit community development corporation assists black entrepreneurs to set up shop and serves as a funnel for Section 502 loans from the Small Business Administration. A Black Land Services program has been developed to halt the loss of land through tax sales and other devices black owners frequently do not understand. Classes and seminars are operating to teach blacks these dangerous mysteries. A small museum on African history operated by Penn Services serves to correct the lies, omissions, and distortions of white history books and curricula and build a can-do attitude among blacks. The museum is located on the grounds of the Penn Services complex at Frogmore, South Carolina.

A veritable clinic is Penn Services. One could go on about OEO cooperatives such as Fruit Cake Delight of Lafayette,

Louisiana, which markets fruitcakes by mail order and a variety of pralines and sugar-cane products. Most cooperatives are developing in the rural South, but strategies for utilizing this movement might be worth considering at this point. Some follow:

1. The federal government should make a policy of strengthening black institutions wherever they exist and work with the black community through them. The antipoverty drive would have been doubly successful if men like Sullivan and Stafford had been involved at the outset.
2. Cooperatives hold great promise for rural areas and small towns in the South where more than one-quarter of the blacks live. Colleges should train blacks like Penn Services' John Gadson to develop cooperatives, and successful co-ops now operating might serve as training grounds for interns from these programs.
3. The federal government might place heavy funding in this movement and use labor mobility projects to relocate some urban blacks for work in these cooperatives. The big problem at this writing is arranging for the continuation of OEO by the Congress. No funds were included in the FY '74 budget by the President. The Congress must act to assure continuation of Penn Services and similar operations by continuing OEO.

Summary

Black youth and adults receive much of their education from a bewildering welter of programs operating under the rubric of continuing education. Because of shabby treatment in some school systems, blacks must rely more on this sort of education than whites. Both groups must rely more on continuing education in the future as economic shifts make new skills desirable and old skills obsolete.

Possibly, school budgets for high-school study in some communities might be reduced and the savings placed in continuing-education programs highly effective with black youth. A situation in which one-half or one-third of black high-school diplomas are received through continuing education might be startling. If this situation represents the best use of funds, continuing education would be entirely desirable.

Every segment of the American community—school, business, industry, churches, and community groups—operates continuing-education programs. The federal government supports much of this effort. An agenda for the black community is to understand as much as possible about this vibrant, dynamic enterprise and drive hard to realize a fair share of the benefits involved.

Notes for Chapter 3

[1] New Careers is a program for paraprofessionals who work in schools, hospitals, and other institutions. The program combines work and further study enabling workers to advance up the career ladder.

[2] Robert Botts, "Profile of a Continuation High School," *Phi Delta Kappan* (May, 1972), pp. 574–76.

[3] *Annual Statistical Report, GED Testing Services,* American Council on Education, Washington, D.C., 1972, p. 1.

[4] *Examiners' Manual for the Tests of General Educational Development,* General Educational Development Service, American Council on Education, Washington, D.C., 1971, p. 2.

[5] *Opportunities for Educational and Vocational Advancement,* Commission of Accreditation of Service Experiences, American Council on Education, Washington, D.C., 1971, pp. 18–19.

[6] U.S. Department of Labor, *Black News Digest,* July 24, 1972, p. 1.

[7] Curtis Ulmer and John Peters, *Training the Paraprofessional* (Monograph) (Englewood Cliffs, N.J.: Prentice-Hall, 1972), p. 1.

[8] U.S. Department of Labor, *Black News Digest,* July 17, 1972, p. 2.

[9] *Annual Report,* National Alliance of Business, Washington, D.C., 1971.

[10] Ibid., p. 23.

[11] *Black News Digest,* op. cit., p. 3.

CHAPTER 4

New Metropolitan Colleges

THE Carnegie Commission on Higher Education has recommended in a special report that fifty four-year colleges and five hundred community colleges be created in our major metropolitan areas by 1976. The need for such colleges to serve city youth was stressed and recommendations for federal financial assistance were outlined.[1]

The Carnegie recommendations are long overdue. Even now, perhaps, the language lacks the urgency to match the situation.

In 1940, for example, 38 percent of white and 12 percent of black young adults (ages twenty-five to twenty-nine) held a high-school diploma. In 1971, this 26-point gap had been narrowed to 17 points with the percentages now only 79 to 62 in favor of whites. Not so for college degrees; the 4-point gap of 1940 (2 percent black, 6 percent white) had risen to 9 points by 1971, with 16 percent of young white adults in this group holding degrees as compared to 7 percent of black black counterparts.[2]

One piece of good news in this scene is the findings in a 1973 study by the Labor Department that white enrollment is declining because of various factors, and this decline, coupled with recent increases in black enrollment, resulted in comparability in the percentage (97) of high-school graduates enrolling in college.

Gaps in Graduate and Professional Study

Graduate and professional study for blacks presents a more severe problem. Less than 3 percent of the practicing physicians in the country are black and only a small percentage of blacks (4.2 percent) are enrolled in medical schools. The same problem exists for law school enrollment with only one black attorney for every 5,000 persons compared to one for every 750 whites, and blacks comprising 3.9 percent of law school enrollment.[3]

White Ph.D. graduation, now exceeding 32,000 annually, has resulted in a surplus and in job difficulties for many. The reverse situation exists for blacks. Only about 4 percent of the total graduate school enrollment is black and Ph.D. production is even lower. Of 37,456 doctorates awarded between 1964 and 1968, only 294 were black (see Figure 14).

The realization of this actual loss of ground was the root cause of many of the actions by black students on college campuses trying to force college administrators to come to grips with the situation. These gentlemen, in turn, simply don't have the resources to make a real dent in the problem of bringing about the needed volume in minority enrollment. Most will do what they can (some will do nothing, of course), but there just isn't enough scholarship money and places in the freshman classes to take the extra students.

To achieve comparability in black-white enrollment, the present estimated enrollment of 485,000 black students in 1970 would have been expanded to 840,000, about 12 percent of the 7 million opening enrollment of fall, 1971. In 1980, 12 million white and 1.5 million black students would be enrolled.[4] Enrollment estimates for 1972–73 made by the Census Bureau are in the neighborhood of 700,000. Recent declines in white enrollment might relieve some of the pressure on blacks to keep pace. Although the numbers seem staggering, almost any black or white campus activist will be quick to point out that mobilization of this sort is treated as child's play when done "in the national interest," say like the draft or defense production. Although the example could be improved, the spirit of the idea deserves consideration. Creating a permanent class of accountants, chemists, teachers, and civil servants in our cities is surely "in the national interest."

Activists and many not too active persons will also impa-

FIGURE 14
MINORITIES IN POSTBACCALAUREATE TRAINING

	Amer. Indian #	%	Black #	%	Oriental #	%	Span-Surn #	%	Total Minority #	%	White-Anglo #	%	Total #	%
Total Grad. & prof. stdts.	1,608	0.3	22,302	4.1	9,662	1.8	6,297	1.2	39,869	7.3	503,281	92.7	543,150	100.0
Non-undergr. med. stdts.	47	0.1	1,845	4.2	789	1.8	363	0.8	3,044	6.9	40,914	93.1	43,958	100.0
Non-undergr. dental stdts.	.21	0.1	597	3.6	296	1.8	127	0.8	1,041	6.2	15,696	93.8	16,737	100.0
Non-undergr. law stdts.	193	0.3	2,552	3.9	317	0.5	702	1.1	3,764	5.8	61,107	94.2	64,871	100.0

SOURCE: James Harvey, "Minorities and Advanced Degrees," *Research Currents*, ERIC Higher Education, June 1, 1972.

tiently dismiss arguments concerning preferential treatment for black people or the rather large sums of money required for such a course of action. The activists quickly point to their belief that restitution is due blacks for labor during the slavery years. Current estimates of the amount due are usually in the neighborhood of $800 billion, far more than enough to enroll an additional 500,000 or so black college students.

Location of Institutions

The logical locations of the institutions would be in cities where cheap or free public education is not available to *all* metropolitan youth or, importantly, where existing public institutions are unable to serve metropolitan youth well. The latter seems odd but probably exists in a larger measure than surface indications. Competition for places has caused some strains. Some whites have complained that the handful of blacks admitted to prestigious institutions were the cause of their not being admitted. This reasoning is difficult to agree with when as many as 8,000 students apply for a thousand places at some universities. Such complaints come dangerously close to scapegoating. Admissions for other ethnic groups are never singled out in this manner or even counted for that matter.

Strangely, calls have come from some Jewish organizations for guards against the reinstitution of ethnic quotas. This call surfaced in the 1972 elections. That American institutions will install the old limits to Jewish enrollment that only recently disappeared is doubtful. Some will use the call, however, to slow their efforts toward development of a sizable black presence in their student populations and a few might also begin anew the subtle ways to discriminate against Jews. Both blacks and Jews would do well to avoid schisms and divisions in traditional alliances involving this sentiment. As the government has made clear in its many pronouncements on the subject, the drive for minority representation in jobs, schools, and housing is built around goals and not quotas. A goal encourages institutions to reach and exceed certain levels. Quotas encourage the reverse.

Even in a time of empty dormitory beds and classrooms at some colleges, a need for colleges in metropolitan areas which will educate black youths and adults in a quiet, systematic way still exists. These schools would not see the need to fill up the newspapers about the noble work they are doing. They would not insult the students with invidious comparisons of College Board scores. They would be quite cognizant of the fact that the 500 median score is a 1941 norm and that the average student takes a lower score with him into college today. Further, because of the lack of cultural specificity in the test, many blacks have already graduated from some of the stronger universities in the country with scores below the 1941 median, and many of these are performing impressive feats in graduate schools or in jobs and businesses.

Keeping in mind the above constraints, a rule-of-thumb estimate might indicate the feasibility of establishing the fifty four-year colleges recommended by the Carnegie Commission in the fifty cities of largest minority group concentrations.

The five hundred community colleges might be located in cities or metropolitan areas with over 25,000 population. Some large cities would benefit from both community and four-year colleges.

A list of cities that might benefit from four-year schools is included below. These cities were chosen because they do not have state colleges available to their populations or because the state colleges in the communities do not serve the black population well.

Albuquerque, N. Mex.
Atlanta, Ga.
Battle Creek, Mich.
Beaumont-Port Arthur, Tex.
Boston, Mass.
Brunswick, Ga.
Buffalo, N.Y.
Cairo, Ill.
Charleston, S.C.

Charlotte, N.C.
Charlottesville, Va.
Chicago, Ill.
Cincinnati, Ohio
Columbus, Ga.
Covington, Ky.
Dallas, Tex.
Danville, Va.
Dayton, Ohio

Denver, Colo.
Dothan, Ala.
El Dorado, Ark.
Evansville, Ind.
Fort Wayne, Ind.
Gary, Ind.
Gasden, Ala.
Grand Rapids, Mich.
Greenville, Miss.
Hartford, Conn.
Hattiesburg, Miss.
Indianapolis, Ind.
Jackson, Mich.
Jackson, Tenn.
Jacksonville, Fla.
Little Rock, Ark.
Los Angeles, Calif.
Louisville, Ky.
Macon, Ga.
Magnolia, Ark.
Mansfield, Ohio
Memphis, Tenn.
Meridian, Miss.
Miami, Fla.
Mobile, Ala.
Muskegon, Mich.
Natchez, Miss.
Newark, N.J.

New Haven, Conn.
New York, N.Y.
Oklahoma City, Okla.
Omaha, Nebr.
Orlando, Fla.
Philadelphia, Pa.
Phoenix, Ariz.
Pittsburgh, Pa.
Poplar Bluff, Mo.
Providence, R.I.
Racine-Kenosha, Wis.
Raleigh, N.C.
Richmond, Va.
Roanoke, Va.
Salt Lake City, Utah
San Antonio, Tex.
San Francisco, Calif.
Seattle, Wash.
Sikeston, Mo.
South Bend, Ind.
St. Louis, Mo.
Tampa, Fla.
Trenton, N.J.
Tulsa, Okla.
Valdosta, Ga.
Vicksburg, Miss.
Wilmington, Del.

If the fifty four-year campuses could enroll an average of 5,000 students each and the five hundred two-year campuses an average of 1,200, both enrollment comparability and efficiency would be served well. Together with expansion of minority enrollment on existing campuses, such an arrangement would yield the 1.08 million minority student population required for enrollment comparability in the 1970s. In 1980, the black full-time enrollment picture might look like the following:

Existing campuses	500,000
Fifty new, 5,000-student, four-year campuses enrolling 3,000 black students each	150,000
Five hundred new, 1,500-student, two-year campuses enrolling an average of 1,000 black students each	500,000
Total black students enrolled	1,150,000
Total students enrolled in new, federally aided colleges	1,000,000
Total black students enrolled in new, federally aided colleges	650,000

The "house plan" of organization for the new colleges might be considered. The four-year schools might consist of five self-contained units for the first two years of work. The two-year students might do all of their work in small houses or schools. This arrangement would be true especially for liberal arts transfer students. The aim is to deliver guidance and diagnostic teaching and to engender the group cohesiveness that seems so necessary to control attrition for this type of student population and graduate a respectable number.

A few paragraphs must be devoted to those who might see the not so fine hand of Milton Henry, leader of the Republic of New Africa, a black separatist group, Strom Thurmond, the separatist senator from South Carolina, and similar separatists in the creation of schools where black students predominate. Such an arrangement need be neither Black Nationalist nor Old South. Blacks predominate among the city people for whom the schools are intended. They will predominate in the student populations and they should predominate in the administration offices, especially the presidencies and student affairs offices. People who have difficulty accepting this proposal might consider the ethnicity of their own school experiences. Southern Baptists, Jews, Methodists, Catholics, Presbyterians—all operate colleges connected to their churches. Very important to remember is wherever these groups have ethnic enclaves or high concentrations of population, they tend to predominate in both the student populations and the administrations of *public colleges*.

Black people feel that only racism of the crudest sort could prompt people to feel that it is somehow wrong for them to predominate or that their schools are inferior if they do. The furor surrounding "racial balance" in schools and neighborhoods triggered the black separatist movement as much as anything. Integration is a two-way street. The unconscious Tarzan complex among many of the most liberal and moderate planners can only yield trouble over the long haul.

A few words might also be said about the role of colleges already operated by blacks in the comparability plan. A considerable degree of confusion has reigned in this area. Predominately black colleges enroll about one-half of the Afro-Americans in college today. Twenty years ago, they enrolled almost everybody of color in American colleges. For one hundred years or so these institutions have struggled under the most adverse conditions, to provide education for this segment of the population. Although three of these schools (Hampton Institute, Tuskegee Institute, and Atlanta University) rank in the top 10 percent of college endowments, the colleges are trying to educate 3 percent of the college population with only 2 percent of the college money.[5] This ridiculous situation should be changed and these schools should be set free.

Freedom in this case should be bought with direct federal subsidies. A yearly subsidy of $30 million would enable these schools to erase the $3,000 salary gap between their 10,000 faculty members and national pay standards. An additional $20 million would enable the colleges to hire an additional 2,500 professors and lower the teaching loads to twelve hours instead of the fifteen hours that is common in too many cases. Subsidies will also bring about comparability in library holdings, science laboratories, and other areas.

The Importance of Scholarship Money

As noted earlier, black students do not go to college because they do not have the money to do so, and black colleges train most of the black professionals and innovators in American life. Economy is the reason for this situation. Black colleges are geared to help poor youth. While the average family income of students in white colleges is about $10,000, black colleges enroll students far below this level and more than one-third attend college on scholarships. Further, twice as many black A and B students (34 percent) must settle for community college.

The importance of the federal scholarship program cannot be overemphasized. The biggest barrier to more black participation in college is the scarcity of scholarship money. Almost every college, black and white, has to turn away students because of this lack. If handled properly, the federal scholarship program contained in the Omnibus Higher Education Bill of 1972 can be a breakthrough. Every prospective college student is assured $1,400 minus what parents are expected to pay with regard to their income. A student from a $15,000-income family qualifies for none of this money and a student from a $6,000-income family qualifies for all of it. Most black college students would qualify for some assistance and many more would be able to attend these schools as well as more white colleges.

The government has a penchant for bad follow-through on good ideas. Possibly, though authorized, enough money will not be appropriated for this program or some committee will write guidelines that will destroy the original intent. This program should be institutionalized as soon as possible, and annual funding should be as automatic as some of the funding done for defense or agricultural subsidies.

Just as important, too, is the title in this bill providing graduate and medical scholarships for minority students. This title provides $3,000 scholarships for about three hundred students per year. Amendments to this bill over the years could assure rapid expansion of scholarship aid in a very vital area. Annual appropriations of $325 million would provide $5,000 scholarships for enough black enrollees in professional and graduate schools (about 65,000) to bring about comparability in this area.

Organization

Twenty major-field departments operating around a common core of general education might serve efficiently for the four-year colleges. A 250-course catalogue might be produced with course proliferation thereafter held to a minimum. The intent would be to help as many students as possible obtain a thorough undergraduate education with the amount of money available. Another way of stating this premise is to say that the schools would be operated for the benefit of the students rather than for the benefit of the faculty. Major course sequences in any given field would be limited to thirty-six semester hours. Salary increments and promotions would be based on teaching and student guidance, as much as on research and writing.

"Grant hustling" would be kept in check. Fulfillment of this goal would require that faculty salaries be above average by perhaps as much as 25 percent. Faculty recruitment and selection procedures would have to develop a faculty with a dedication to undergraduate instruction.

Such dedication might seem impossible considering the domination of higher education by the graduate schools, the research associations, and the federal grants community—but pendulums swing. If the teachers were paid well and if the average research efforts were blended with teaching with students participating heavily and learning in the process, one would expect results. For the huge research projects some faculties are bound to want to take on, a nonprofit firm might be formed with space and equipment leased from the colleges. The professors would take leave from the school and would not have to pretend to be teaching.

Graduate students from other colleges could come aboard as full-time researchers. They, too, would not have to pretend to teach anybody. Put differently, one might say that the students would not have to subsidize research efforts by receiving most of their instruction from people who do not have their minds on teaching. By frankly renting their labs and shops to the entrepreneurs for a profit, the colleges could also avoid the indirect cost lag. Under such an arrangement, the duplication of the Harvard experience of having seven thousand "teachers" for fourteen thousand students would be impossible. Research would be done and teaching would not suffer, however.

Afro-American Studies

Afro-American and Third-World studies would find a place in the curriculum without argument. A twelve-course major built around a common liberal arts–general education core would be the pattern. Heavy emphasis on economics and community development might predominate in these majors, as well as in other majors. The teacher-training program, for example, should take off in an entirely new direction. According to the recent report of the American Association of Colleges for Teacher Education, the whole setup is beyond repair and the only hope is a complete new start. Urban-education departments in the new colleges could lead the way. Still in this vein, departments of engineering, psychology, sociology, economics, political science, and business administration would all seem to offer unusual potential for serving as catalyzing and vitalizing forces in the local metropolitan scene. If these projections come through as they should, future black politicians, businessmen, real estate operators, urban-renewal specialists, and social workers would pour from these colleges in well-trained droves. The present often dismal scramble for the "qualified Negro" would become but a dim memory.

Outreach Programs

A vital division in the new colleges should be urban extension. As in the case of the new Federal City College in Washington, D.C., Congress might declare all of the four-year colleges urban land-grant colleges and provide funds for them to duplicate the feats and accomplishments of their rural counterparts. Efforts to reach such competence, seemingly, can take off in almost any direction. Rural agents under the supervision of the state land-grant colleges will assist a farmer to get federal money to create a lake, stock it with fish, and charge people to fish in it. Women learn how to make jelly, combat insects, and worm a horse. How to grow more vegetation on less acreage is taught by work, deed, and a steady rain of literature. How to collect from the government for the steady accumulation of surplus land proceeds in the same manner. Paralleling these rural agent activities, the urban agent program would include facts on how to get a better job, open a business, assure city services for the community, and raise children. Imagine what would be generated if 70 professional "urban agents" were operating in Roxbury, Massachusetts, under the aegis of the new Douglass-Sumner College—or 150 agents at King-McGill in Atlanta.

Transitional Studies

Now to the part that so many detractors from the idea have been waiting so patiently to see treated: the remedial program for those poor unwashed students for whom they may consider this whole spending scheme a misuse of taxpayers' money— money that might eradicate an apartheid caste system and loose hordes of black, educated applicants for their (the detractors) jobs, housing developments, and even for cosignatures on the marriage licenses of their sisters and sons. And besides, what is going to happen to that therapeutic social-class pyramid if black youth crack the base asunder? Who will be around to feel sorry for or better than? Will there be no standards?

To paraphrase the English program chairman of a social event: "Are we not to exclude anyone, and thus end up with nothing?" Hardly.

To begin with, the exclusion of a remedial program from the four-year colleges and a different label for it in the two-year schools would be best. The *transitional studies program* is a suggestion. The terms *culturally deprived, culturally dis-*

advantaged, culturally unique, disadvantaged, socially disad-
vantaged, educationally deprived, slum students, ghetto
youngsters, risk students, project students, and similar connota-
tions would be declared taboo in the new colleges. These
phrases are too often the new language of prejudice and they
cause nothing but trouble. Unfortunately, the public schools
cannot seem to exorcise the categories from their midst. Labeling students *project students* is the root cause of much of the
black separatism on college campuses.

Instead, these brave new schools would be urban land-grant
colleges with a special interest in first generation college students, many of whom come from families with modest to moderate incomes and whose school systems may not have been
as strong as some. A good strong reader with recommendations
from almost anybody about his academic promise would be
enrolled in the four-year schools. Poor readers and late bloom-
ers would be enrolled in transitional studies and transfer programs at the two-year schools. The experiences of community
colleges with programmed learning and mechanical teaching devices would be built upon in these programs. Money should be
made available to take every student with promise. If room were
not available in the day freshmen class, the student could either
attend the twilight shift or enroll in a day summer semester, take
a night fall semester and take the place of a day dropout or
transfer student in the winter semester. For many students, of
course, and these young people may be bright or dull, the
colleges may suggest that they plan careers without college
attendance. The new national emphasis on career education
will facilitate this move.

Through the general education curriculum and the social
sciences, business, and education majors, the colleges would
have the opportunity to develop institutions that will serve
metropolitan communities well. A one-year course in metropolitan civilizations, for example, might replace the old Western
civilization courses that now often repeat dates, wars, people,
and places learned in high school.

The new course would enable the student to understand factors and events that have brought cities to their present state.

A course in metropolitan political processes should develop the informed city councilmen, mayors, school board, and planning commission members so important in metropolitan vitality. Humanities courses would be frank about the dehumanizing aspects of the city. A capstone course in metropolitan planning might try to pull all aspects of the above areas together somewhere at the junior or senior year level.

Pitfalls on the Road to Success

Many pitfalls can hamper progress in establishing these institutions. Some obstacles will be especially difficult such as developing a receptive climate in the Congress in preparation for legislation and appropriations for the schools. However, with the Carnegie Commission, American Council on Education, and American Association for Higher Education joining forces with traditional black and liberal organizations, this climate can be developed over a period of three to five years.

If a pattern of annual appropriations could be established, the problem of federal support becomes solvable. One might say the valves of the financial pipelines have been opened. The government already operates two colleges administered and attended by blacks. The government also supports a college for deaf students, military colleges, over a thousand military installations including a vast educational system and several staff colleges. The land-grant college setup has already been mentioned and one could mention other federal schools for post-secondary education. The point to be made is that no precedent-shattering event will take place if federal support is extended to a network of colleges serving both city youth and American cities. Quite to the contrary, such a move is the most logical expenditure the country could make at this time.

Administrators, faculties, and news media have a job to do that is mainly psychological—the development and projection to themselves, the students, the academic community, and the public of a concept of excellence different from the inadequate concepts that so hamper higher educational processes in this country.

Unfortunately, many college faculty and administrators have a herd instinct that sets them up for most fads coming down the pike. Further, the leadership seems to suffer from an expansion syndrome. Given a meeting of two college presidents (or a president and a reporter) at any point in time, one would more than likely hear the conversation begin with "how many"— how many students, how many buildings, how many books, how many dollars in current fund expenditures, how many teachers, how many Ph.D.'s, how many federal grants, how many federal research projects, how many games won, how many articles and books written, how many points on the SAT, how many on the graduate record, how many students to graduate school? Then, for lack of another method of exhibiting good stewardship, "how much" the educators plan to expand the "how many" would occupy the second block of time in the conversation.

Undergraduate higher education should be on a higher plane. The new colleges have an opportunity to make such a wish come true. However, these institutions will run a great risk of being led into this quantitative treadmill.

Better Ratings Standards

The challenge is not to return to the old days when the college was viewed as a sort of monastic retreat, where a chosen few could reflect and absorb in preparation for national and world leadership. The challenge is not so much a matter of changing the white thrusts of the American college, which surely the black students will try to accomplish. The problem rests in defining what a metropolitan college of this type should be trying to do with, to, and for its students and community. Once this question is answered, parsing out both quantities and qualities of excellence can proceed.

Presidents and trustee boards of the new colleges would have a grave responsibility for making clear the new concepts of excellence to a great many persons if the colleges are to be allowed to grow in such a direction. Or, indeed, if they are to avoid deep conflict and are allowed to grow at all. The nub of the problem seems to be what more than one observer has noted as a peculiar penchant for Americans constantly to try to achieve social mobility through their jobs and institutions. Therefore, if reason does not prevail, many people will be unhappy and fail to work for excellence within the framework of stated goals of the institutions if the community colleges are not moving toward four-year status, if the four-year schools are not moving toward new Ph.D. programs and institutes for advanced study, if the athletic program is not moving toward bigtime operations replete with bowl games.

All of these inclinations can be avoided and new concepts of excellence clearly enunciated to new faculty prospects, the press, and the community by the president and his deans. The first two years would be very important in setting the image and mold for the future of the colleges.

The importance of being candid cannot be overemphasized. The trustee board must be candid with the presidential candidate about the role and future of the school. If he were led to believe that he would be able truthfully to insinuate at the American Council on Education meetings that he is building another Ohio State, conflict will surely ensue, the school won't grow apace, and the man will eventually have to be fired. The deans and the president must be candid with the faculty candidates. A large measure of the unhappiness on the campuses of four-year colleges with moderate admissions standards can be traced to faculty recruiters who led prospects to believe that they would be able to attend the meetings of their professional associations and talk about "my graduate students" and "my research grants" and "my practically nonexistent teaching load" and "my ability to avoid freshmen." Recruits should not believe that all classes would be at 10:00 A.M. in the room next door to the teacher's office and that all undergraduate students would write and reason at roughly the master's degree level.

The academic community would also have a grave responsibility for promoting the acceptability and good image of the new schools.

The Job at Hand

Now is surely the time to rally around the idea of creating new federal colleges in metropolitan areas. Black American youths will be brought into the college-trained work force in a fair share of numbers.

Again, the biggest and most exploited minority in America is owed a considerable amount in the way of reparations payments. Achieving comparability in the college-trained work force and plying vigorously the idea of metropolitan land-grant colleges might be one method of paying part of this debt.

Notes for Chapter 4

[1] Carnegie Commission on Higher Education, *Quality and Equality: New Levels of Federal Responsibility for Higher Education* (Hightstown, N.J.: McGraw-Hill Book Co., 1969), p. 4.

[2] U.S. Office of Education, *Digest of Educational Statistics,* 1968, p. 9.

[3] James Harvey, "Minorities and Advanced Degrees," *Research Currents* (June 1, 1972), ERIC Higher Education Center.

[4] U.S. Office of Education, op. cit., p. 11.

[5] Earl McGrath, *The Predominately Negro Colleges and Universities in Transition* (New York: Teachers College Press, 1965), p. 27.

CHAPTER 5

Eliminating Strategic Errors
in Plans and Programs

To HOPE that the planning and development of programs to assist in the development of poor children and youth could proceed without some errors in strategy and programs is perhaps too optimistic. More than a fair share of these errors occurred and valuable time and energy had to be expended in correcting them.

Through careless planning and execution in the area of measurement and evaluation, the long dormant nature-nurture debate was reignited, and white supremacists who always come to this scene reappeared to spew again their vitriol.[1]

Ironically, the argument over heredity versus environment is mainly over 30 percentage points. One small band contends that heredity accounts for 80 percent of one's intellect, a much larger group insists that environment and heredity account for 50 percent each, and two tiny groups of hardliners claim 100 percent for their side. The argument would be amusing if so many poor children had not been injured by the atmosphere of doubt and mistrust of their capabilities created by newspaper sensationalism.

Possibly another gene-pool argument will not emerge. The abrasive leadership of the white supremacists has sparked a remarkable reaction among researchers. Ample evidence has been marshaled to explode the theories advanced. Much of what has been proposed will hurt whites as much as blacks. These proposals have caused concern in the white community. The make-up of the leadership cadres is also odd. The top man is an engineer who has decided to devote his last years to eugenics. His most bizarre proposal is the sterilization of everyone with an IQ under 100—half the American population. A colleague is an educational psychologist whose book on the deleterious effects of environment on intellect was released a few months before his article in a student-sponsored journal discounted the effects of environment on intellect.

A limited amount of scientific knowledge about intellect, its origins and its measurement, is available. In spite of excessive speculation about genetic influences on intellect, geneticists know very little about genes and how they operate on anything. Psychologists know even less. Yet, a difference between the two scientists is noted. Geneticists know that they do not know and are quick to point this out. A small number of psychologists do not seem endowed with either the insight or the virtue under discussion.

Exactly one gene has been isolated and examined at its work as a control mechanism for bodily functions. This gene was studied in a one-cell organism having to do with sugar metabolism in yeast. Whether a gene or combination of genes having to do with intellect will be isolated and studied remains to be seen. The gene stands as one of the unsolved mysteries of science.

Scientists are still unable to state unequivocally how people learn and remember things or how they think. Whether or not scientists will ever be able to say exactly what happens in the learning process remains to be seen. Closely related to these phenomena is the most enigmatic organ of all: the brain. This fascinating mass of nerves and tissue contains ten billion nerve cells that control thought and action. All brains look alike, and scientists know almost next to nothing about how the brain really works, how it operates in the thinking process, and how it stores knowledge once it is gained. Some interesting research is going forward on the biochemistry and electrochemistry of the brain, but the research is in a crude stage at best.

Congress should legislate a law requiring all writers and

editors to describe the state of the art of psychological research when embarking upon lofty discussions involving psychological and psychophysiological phenomena. Even wide and contentious disagreement on the definition of intellect abounds. A good companion law would require large labels on commercial tests stating that they do not purport to measure innate abilities.

A Remarkable People

A word or two about minority capabilities might be appropriate. Most headlines are generated by invidious speculation regarding differences in IQ scores of blacks and whites. Thirty percent of the blacks score higher on these tests than 50 percent of the whites. In a perfect world, 50 percent of the blacks would score higher than 50 percent of the whites. But the world is imperfect. Then indeed, blacks may be superior to whites to achieve in this manner given the isolation and handicaps they have endured. Whatever, blacks are a remarkable people and but for the reluctance of writers to bring out the facts, more of this story would be widely known.

Consider the fact, for example, that in spite of 350 years of the most inhuman treatment other than in Nazi Germany, blacks in America have managed to multiply themselves by a factor of six.

In the first fifty years after emancipation from slavery, black inventors filed over one thousand patents, although less than a hundred high schools and almost no colleges were open to them during this period. Blacks have filed over three thousand patents since the inception of the U.S. Patent Office, including the design or development of the stoplight, vanilla extract, the gas mask, the shoe last, blood plasma, plastics, peanut butter, ice cream, and potato chips.

A black scientist born a slave and raised by Iowa whites revolutionized a boll weevil-ridden Southern agriculture with the development of new products from soybeans and peanuts, and black engineers developed the airframe for rockets, which eliminated the need for second- and third-stage engines, and developed the ejection seat for jet fighter planes.[2] A black scientist won the 1972 NASA Distinguished Achievement Award for development of the lunar observatory for the expeditions to the moon. Another black genius played a big role in designing our nation's capitol. A black surgeon performed the first open-heart operation. A black physician developed the blood bank. In Olympic competition, blacks are six times more likely than whites to win a gold medal.

Although the two top IQ tests include no blacks and no Southeastern individuals in their norm groups, blacks who are so disposed and who have access to good schools do well on them. The highest scoring school in Los Angeles in 1969 was 90 percent black.[3] Black soldiers in World War II outscored whites from several states.[4] Black draftees from a Northwestern state outscored white draftees in all Southern states and several Northern states in 1970.[5]

About forty black students win National Merit Scholarships each year, and since racial restrictions were eased in 1969, about three Rhodes Scholars have been selected from black collegians each year.

As has been shown in Chapter 1, blacks nearly doubled both their high-school graduation and college entrance rates in the last five years. Significant gains were also made in income and housing.

A number of major comparability studies show blacks matching whites on IQ tests. Some results show blacks outstripping whites on these tests. A description of some of these studies follows. Important to note is that in most of the latter cases the subjects were from black middle-class homes in communities with good schools. Special high-impact programs, however, produced an above normal spread of test scores to children in depressed areas. Most studies show comparability, that is, middle-class blacks matching middle-class whites and blacks and whites in depressed areas coming up short.

A Virginia State Board of Education study showed a black school leading the state in reading in 1970.[6]

Rick Heber, a specialist in learning disabilities at the University of Wisconsin, showed average and above average IQ scores in a five-year longitudinal experiment with black ghetto children.[7]

A. J. Mayeske, a USOE statistician, grouped the Coleman Report data according to social class and found black-white comparability.[8]

Siegfried Englemann, a University of Oregon education professor, shows average and above average IQ scores in a variety of projects with black ghetto children.[9]

Jane Mercer, a sociologist at the University of California at Riverside, found black-white comparability in a study of 125,000 schoolchildren grouped according to social class.[10]

A National Merit Scholarship study of black recipients of its awards—about 40 a year—showed that average ability scores exceeded the ninety-eighth percentile on national norms.[11]

Franklin Brown, a University of Minnesota psychologist, found black-white comparability for samples matched for social class in Minneapolis schools.[12] McCord and Demmarath of Boston University found the same results for children in Boston.[13] McQueen and Churn of the University of Nevada found the same for Nevada children.[14]

Eyferth, a German psychologist, found no difference in IQs of German children of black soldiers and their all-German counterparts.[15]

Paul Witty, an expert on gifted children, has documented extensively the capacities of a black student who made the highest score ever on IQ tests.[16]

Some insights are available for American history buffs: black slaves who turned on their Spanish masters in a party exploring the Pee Dee River Valley of South Carolina were the first permanent settlers in America. The Spaniards folded their tents and left and the blacks stayed on. The year was 1526, nearly one hundred years before the landing of the Mayflower.[17]

The litanies of white supremacists would fall on deafer ears than they do now if the media and academics would do a better job of writing the facts. There is an unrecognized problem here, or at least a problem that has not been faced squarely. The sad but simple fact is that white writers are reluctant to write about blacks who excel. Sports writers seem to have gotten over this hang-up, although Jack Johnson is still not in some encyclopedias. Academic writers have a long way to go, however. Maybe the future will bring some breakthroughs.

Hereditary Aristocracy

Another rather confusing theory advanced by one or two psychologists holds that the country has evolved to a point in the development of talent that a hereditary aristocracy exists. According to these theorists, no longer can the children of poor people possibly work their way up the ladder of success. Everyone who inherited the ability to climb this ladder has already climbed it and only their children are worthy of quality education, access to good jobs, and kind treatment by the moneylenders.

All of this assertion is inaccurate, of course, and in the final analysis, un-American. The theory also affects millions of whites and has received negative responses from all quarters.

Little needs to be said about this theory except to point out that some of the most ordinary talent is found in the offspring of some of our more affluent families and that American working-class families still produce an outsize share of our gifted children. Proponents of the hereditary aristocracy will not get very far with this theory, and the wrath of many American people will be brought down upon them if attempts are made to shape policy on this basis.

Affluent families do send more children to college than working-class families and keep them there longer. However, the careful schooling and financial support afforded these students play a large role here. The National Academy of Sciences noted in a nature-nurture statement in its January, 1971, annals of proceedings that a carefully trained youngster with modest endowments will often outstrip a brilliant, but shabbily educated counterpart. Affluent children are afforded the best education money can buy and almost all are sent to college whether they want to go or not. Further, there are colleges operating in America that almost any student can enter regardless of academic promise. Again, the hereditary aristocracy is not yet prevalent in America and probably will not be in the foreseeable future.

Black ghetto children and whites in similar circumstances have tremendous potential for development. Lester Wheeler studied Tennessee mountain whites over a ten-year period during which schools were improved drastically and the TVA brought jobs and income to the area.[18] The increase in test scores, high-school graduation rates, and college attendance was just as spectacular. As noted previously, Rick Heber enrolled black ghetto children in Milwaukee in a cradle school at the age of five days and achieved good results. Siegfried Englemann, also mentioned previously, has a high-impact program for K-3, which he operates out of the University of Oregon for about one hundred school systems enrolling black ghetto children. These schools are scattered across the country. His IQ and achievement scores are just as spectacular as Heber's. David Weikart operates a similar program called High Scope out of Ypsilanti, Michigan.

In short, poor children can learn. If they do not learn, growing evidence indicates that timidity or the lack of know-how or the lack of will on the part of the school system plus the lack of parental push prevents them from doing so.

The Government as Part of the Problem

The federal government is as responsible as any bigot for generating nature-nurture arguments that do violence to minorities. A strange business, the procedure goes something like this: First, liberal members of Congress develop a program and appropriate monies to improve the schooling of the poor. Second, the Office of Education and the Office of Child Development mount these programs. Third, an outside firm is retained to evaluate the program and proceeds to make a negative report based on biased tests of areas not stressed by the program. Fourth, strangely, the government asks for more money so it can really get the job done. Fifth, genetic elitists come forward with loud claims that failure is proof that poor children and particularly poor minority children cannot learn.

One finds little hope that this dismal process will be changed or that government people will even be able to grasp the fact that they are part of the problem. This writer asked an Office of Education official why he always painted such a grim picture of minority education and why he never reported any successes. He was told that if grim pictures were not painted and if successes were reported, congressmen and their constituencies would feel that everything was all right and that there was no need for educational appropriations to improve minority schooling. How do you handle a mentality of this sort?

A better way of doing things in this area has got to be found. People will be needed to convince the government to report and build on successes of their efforts and to do everything possible to avoid deepening the stereotypes they ostensibly set out to erase. Time and a lot of effort will tell. However, this writer is not optimistic.

Schools and Universities as Parts of the Problem

The nineteen thousand school systems in America and the colleges and universities that train and retrain their teachers and administrators are parts of the problem. School testing is a $300-million-a-year enterprise involving several large corporations. Some of these schools are either too inept or too timid to stop giving invalid tests to minorities. However, many schools have reformed these practices. The universities train school people to commit this offense, and professors and test corporation consultants seem too smug and self-satisfied to take leadership roles in changing a bad situation.

The two most hallowed tests in American psychometrics (Stanford-Binet and Wechsler) include no minorities in their norm populations and no items sampled from minority culture in their makeup. One was standardized in California, from where one-half of its 4,400 children came, most from suburban towns and villages. When racists and genetic elitists assemble the now-tattered studies showing whites outscoring minorities on tests, they are reporting data from these tests and others like them that have been collected mostly in school-system testing programs. Further, many of these "studies" were completed by university professors or their graduate students working for advanced degrees. Oddly, many results were collected by minorities themselves at the behest of their mentors—a sad situation.

Bringing needed reforms is going to be difficult. Money, prestige, and power are all involved. A government educational-industrial complex syndrome even exists. The federal government provides funds to keep the engine running through its National Defense Education Act and Elementary and Secondary Education Act programs.

School systems should eliminate IQ testing except for special cases or on request of parents or students. Culture-specific tests should be available for minorities as they are for majorities in IQ testing. Criterion-referenced tests should replace norm-based achievement tests.

Persuasion and pressure from both community and educational leadership on both test corporations and the schools that use these instruments will be necessary to bring about the needed change. Such needed reform will not readily come.

The Future

What could a man offer as strategy for a group of people in a country where the government, the universities, the schools, and many evil people seemed to be arrayed against them in a particular instance? Many things can be done, and black and other minority people are forging ahead in spite of many obstacles.

The black and other minority communities must rally to eliminate IQ testing from the schools they attend. IQ test elimination has been done in New York City, Philadelphia, and many other cities, and concerted effort will get these tests out of the measurement programs everywhere.

Every stratagem will be employed by school systems in some

instances to avoid dropping these tests. Correction formulas will be belatedly proffered, local and ethnic norms will be suggested, and some schools will come up with culture-specific tests. Any good that can come from an IQ test will surely be outweighed by the bad, however.

Thousands of minority children are denied equal access to quality education each year because of flaws in the testing apparatus. This situation is illegal, immoral, and untenable. At least twenty class-action suits seeking to force school districts to cease and desist in the inaccurate testing of minority children have been filed in various parts of the country. The biggest suit was filed in December 1971, in a federal district court by black and Chicano groups seeking dissolution of all classes for the retarded in California.

The problems minority children run into involving testing begin the day the child first comes to the school and is administered an imprecise test. His score is recorded on his cumulative record to follow him like an albatross throughout his school career. Teachers will not work diligently with children who have less than a score of 100 recorded on their cumulative folders, and this first grader receives less than his share of attention and assistance.

As the child moves through the school, he can be sure he will receive less than his share of rewards and reinforcements, receive more than his share of slights and indignities, be denied access to a curriculum that might prepare him for college, and be given a fond good-bye if he should decide to drop out.

More people are losing confidence in the schools; the spectacle of a testing apparatus in disarray will do little to restore this confidence. The $300-million testing industry will simply have to come up with some better instruments; the schools will have to eliminate those instruments detrimental to the well-being of the child, and psychometrists and teachers will have to retrain themselves in a more sophisticated use of tests to insure that the measurements become a part of the solution instead of part of the problem in American schools.

Resistance to this movement will come from test consultants who have advised the industry for many years, schoolteachers and administrators who are resistant to change, racists who see their last hope for white supremacy going down the drain, professors who have taught future and in-service teachers to make these mistakes, and those in the psychometric profession who will try to justify these mistakes. Reform is long overdue and the beginnings now being witnessed will accelerate and result in a better situation.

Henry Dyer, who served as vice president of the Educational Testing Service and is the acknowledged dean of American psychometrists, has noted that IQ tests are the most useless source of educational controversy ever invented and that schools that have not dropped them from their testing programs should do so forthwith. Dyer notes that most of our older distinguished Americans have never had an IQ test because they came through schools too poor to give one or they were enrolled before the tests became widespread. Dyer said that a more sophisticated testing apparatus can be developed for schools with a heterogeneous population but that continuation of IQ tests would preclude this development. Again, sophisticated strategies for eliminating these studies are known and can be used by concerned communities.

Minorities might also take steps to reduce the number of children in poor families. Children in large families with modest incomes simply cannot get the type of development they need in a technological world. Parents need $35,000 to raise a child and give him a high-school education, $40,000 if he goes to a state college. Poor families have made the decision to stunt their children's growth when they decide to have more than one or two. Abortion upon demand is only easily accessible in one or two states and family planning devices are not widely available to poor people.

Further in this vein, small families have brighter children on the average. A widely recognized first-child syndrome exists, which, incidentally, has never been controlled for in the shabby studies on black-white comparability or any comparison studies for that matter. First-born and only children outscore other children by a large margin. Two-thirds of the National Merit Scholars and two-thirds of the Ivy League students are first-born or only children. Excepting middle-class blacks, white first-born and only children will be proportionately higher on scholastic measurement than blacks and will skew the results of comparisons. This writer has never seen a single reference to this simple fact in any studies of black-white comparability. Like biased tests, examiner-examinee rapport, and home background, size of family has simply never been controlled for. Correction formulas applied to the data from these studies might very well show blacks statistically ahead instead of behind whites.

Black communities might also emphasize a different slant on infant education, both at home and in cradle, nursery, and prekindergarten schools, and therein lies the key to a certain type of thinking and reasoning that is valued and needed in technological societies. Many blacks think there is something wrong with white people and will be reluctant to subject their children to a way of thinking and reasoning they regard as white and potentially harmful. This reasoning by blacks can be overcome by skillful explanations of the potential benefits to be gained.

Skills presently revered as highly intellectual in industrial societies are verbal facility and the skill in discerning differences, recognizing similarities, and generalizing from this information. Children who learn these skills internalize them as habits and are served well by them in learning the symbolic language and tasks of the school curriculum. The credentials from the schools get them into jobs in the corporate-industrial state. Sheer ability to survive in a hostile environment, say, as a Louisiana nutria trapper, is perhaps a better measure of intellect for some students. However, verbal skills and abstract reasoning are a major part of the industrial game and minorities are going to have to play it.

Problems of regionalism will be inevitable. Southern blacks and many Northerners with Southern heritages do not hold excessive verbalism and abstractions in high regard. Like their white counterparts in or from this region, these Southern-oriented individuals have traditionally raised their children to be seen and not heard, and if called upon to speak, to be as brief, direct, and straightforward as possible. Abstract verbal gymnastics are regarded as little more than rationalized duplicity (which they sometimes are) and are discouraged. To reform education, all of these concepts and preconceptions have to somehow change in the new scheme of things.

Black working-class families can join with working-class whites to substitute criterion-referenced tests for normative-based achievement tests in the schools. These two groups are locked in a struggle they are bound to lose where norm-based tests are concerned. When the average norm-group scores for almost any given test are grouped according to occupation of parent, white-collar children comprise the upper one-half of the group and blue-collar the lower. In order for the high-scoring white-collar child to succeed, the blue-collar child must fail in the normative-based game. When children in working-class areas score lower than white-collar areas, they are simply reflecting the way the game was structured. White-collar children must stand on blue-collar shoulders to succeed.

If all the working-class children scored at or above the average, the entire system would collapse simply because a normative scale needs a lower base on which to rest. An alternative that the test companies would probably take would be to make the test harder and shorten the time, thereby again putting distance between the washed and the unwashed and maintaining a "normal" curve. The washed are not without suffering in this process. Parents and teachers must push the youngsters even harder to keep them from falling off the treadmill and below the average—a fate worse than death. This brand of parental pushing is done only to the detriment of the children's mental well-being.

Criterion-referenced tests give a better and saner method of doing business. What we really want to know is whether or not standards have been set for the children's schooling, whether these standards are clear and attainable, and whether the children did indeed attain them.

Dyer suggests a rapid expansion of the new school programs based on the philosophy of the great Swiss psychologist, Jean Piaget. In the Piagetian school, teachers, tests, and the curriculum are all viewed as resources to ascertain the stages of development for each child and to develop a program that would maximize his development.

Instead of being slapped in the face with a biased IQ test, the child would receive a sophisticated battery of tests designed to ascertain his stages of development in language, conservation, symbol manipulation, discriminant analysis, and other skills. None of the results are recorded in the cumulative folder, and the teacher uses them as a base from which to work with the child and help him grow and develop his capabilities. To measure progress, criterion-referenced tests are used instead of the norm-based achievement tests. The pressure of child-racing is eliminated for all children, and growth is expected toward clear and friendly standards instead of a struggle to clamber across some median on a normative-based test.

In the Piagetian school, parent conferences and skill sheets replace report cards, and continuous progress learning replaces promotion from grade to grade. The schools do not have any grades.

If the teacher has young charges in her room who live in distinctive cultures, she might resort to culture-specific tests to assess the stages of development of the child. Familiar symbols of the neighborhood are used to ascertain the child's ability to manipulate symbolically or to think. A Mississippi Delta child, for example, might be asked to match singletrees, lespedezas, sweetmilk, tedders, dashers, hame straps, blueticks, and walkers instead of sonatas or bas-reliefs. The factors of geography and life-styles are eliminated in environment testing. The actual content of any test is irrelevant in the Piagetian school; the thinking process is the prime requisite in ascertaining the starting point in any school program.

Culture-specific tests are not new. The corporations have found developing a test for all forty or so distinctive American cultural groups simply unprofitable. The government or school systems or both should make this development possible in a few years. Until that time schools, school systems, or individual teachers can make their own tests. No great mystery should surround test making. Over ten thousand tests are on the market. One of this writer's colleagues marketed and has made $5,000 on a test that he prepared and sold by mail from his office. Like the early struggle to get publishers to market integrated textbooks, this movement will probably have to resort to teacher and school-system efforts to prime the pump. When the interests of the stockholders can be served, the test corporations will move into the field with gusto.

The situation where criterion-referenced tests are concerned is somewhat better. These are achievement tests that measure exactly what has been taught—in a particular module or unit, by a particular teacher, in a particular time span. Many of the new module programs like DISTAR and Individually Prescribed Instruction come replete with criterion-referenced tests.

Again, the value is the removal of time and child-racing as variables. The latter is a game that working-class family children are not likely ever to win and one that places a lot of stress on children from white-collar families. Criterion-referenced tests eliminate the need to have losers in the testing game for some in the group to succeed. Criterion-referenced tests focus on growth and behaviorally oriented goals. When the child reaches these goals he is considered educated. Scrambling to the post faster than the kid in the seat across the aisle is not considered a worthy goal, but thoroughness and the ability to do both convergent and divergent thinking on the topic studies are rewarded.

Notes for Chapter 5

[1] The nature-nurture debate has been with the educational sector for many years and seems insoluble. The theory involves the relative importance of environment and heredity in the development of human abilities—a chicken or the egg argument.

[2] *Legacy for All: A Record of Achievement by Black American Scientists,* Western Electric Corporation, New York, 1970.

[3] Eli Ginsburg, *The Negro Potential* (New York: Columbia University Press, 1960).

[4] Olive Walker, "The Windsor Hills School Story," *Integrated Education* (May–June, 1970), p. 4.

[5] Department of the Army, *Health of the Army Supplement: Results of Examination of Youths for Military Service,* 1971, pp. 138–39.

[6] Virginia State Board of Education, *Test Score Reports, City and County Districts,* 1971.

[7] S. P. Strickland, "Can Slum Children Learn," *American Education* (July, 1971).

[8] A. J. Mayeske, "Minority Achievement" (Paper presented at the 1971 Conference of the American Psychological Association, Washington, D.C.).

[9] U.S. Office of Education, *It Works: A Report on Illinois Academic Primary Programs,* 1968.

[10] Jane Mercer, "Minority IQ" (Paper presented at 1971 Conference of the American Psychological Association, Washington, D.C.).

[11] *Outstanding Negro High School Graduates,* National Merit Scholarship Corporation Research Reports, 1969.

[12] Franklin Brown, "An Experimental and Critical Study of the Intelligence of Negro and White Children," *Journal of Genetic Psychology* 15 (1944), pp. 161–75.

[13] W. M. McCord and N. J. Demmarath, "Negro Versus White Intelligence, A Continuing Controversy," *Harvard Educational Review,* 28 (1958), pp. 120–35.

[14] R. McQueen and B. Churn, "The IQ and Educational Achievements of a Matched Sample of Negro and White Children," *School and Society* 88 (1960), pp. 327–29.

[15] K. Eyferth, "Eine Unterschung der Neger Mischelingkinder," *Vita Humana* 2 (1959), pp. 102–14.

[16] V. Thomas and P. Witty, "Case Studies and Genetic Records of Gifted Negroes," *Journal of Psychology* 15 (1943), pp. 165–81.

[17] Phillip T. Drotning, *Black Heroes in Our Nation's History* (New York: Cowles Book Co., 1969), pp. 5–6.

[18] Lester Wheeler, "A Comparative Study of the Intelligence of East Tennessee Mountain Children," *The Journal of Educational Psychology* (May, 1972), pp. 322–33.

CHAPTER 6

Agenda for Business, Government, and School People

A DISCUSSION follows concerning strategies for assuring the continuation of the momentum surrounding the education of black Americans during the 1960s and early 1970s and strategies for generating success in areas of need. Federal, state, and local governments will take initiatives, and more businesses and industries are managing to see their roles and assume them. Schools are defined as all levels of education from cradle schools to study for the Ph.D. The performance of the black community is so crucial that a separate chapter is given over to its role.

So many fronts exist in education on which to deploy forces and resources that many Americans find it difficult to conceptualize coherent strategies. The American mind looks for short-term breakthroughs and panaceas to problems. Less simple solutions elude the American grasp and cause discouragement and dismay. Generals in the struggle may fruitfully spend an unusual amount of time explaining both the battle plan and the ground won over time. The troops, as well as the citizens, can benefit from this focus.

The problem of coursing off in too many directions comes to mind. Andrew Brimmer, the black Federal Reserve Board member, has complained that the black community is often adrift in a sea of projects, nostrums, innovations, new ideas, experiments, and the brainstorms of short-run politicians. Literally thousands of things *can* be done to assure quality education to blacks. The challenge is to select a general thrust plus the twenty or thirty most promising components of this thrust, and hammer away with the critical mass of energy and resources necessary to drive the enterprise forward.

A general thrust of consolidating gains and spurring successes in areas of need would indicate the need for old components dealing with school funding, housing, jobs, community involvement, and undergraduate scholarships. The need is to make these programs more effective through increased funding, more effective management, new techniques, or through a combination of all of these. New components dealing with scholarships for graduate and professional study, new measurement needs, counterproductive research, job banks, development of major black universities, and varied black business schemes also must be added to a coherent strategy. Also needed are clearly defined, high-yielding fronts on which industry, government, and school people must rally their forces.

School Funding

Schools many black children attend are not funded properly. Too little money is available for a good program and blacks are taxed too heavily to raise it. Like many whites, blacks in many communities might pay $1,200 a year in taxes on a $20,000 home and find that the community is unable to come near the $1,000 per child spent in the average school system in the country or the $1,500 per child spent in the very best. The tax money spent from meager budgets leaves little left over for the enriched home life so important in education. More ominous, tiny school budgets simply will not provide for top-notch teachers and facilities. The former are off in greener pastures and construction and equipment costs preclude the latter. Bland County, Virginia, a mostly white community, raises less than $500 a year per child for its children, although it ranks near the top of the state in taxes paid by its families. The results are devastating. Fifty-two percent of Bland's teachers have not finished college. The libraries are substandard. School buildings leave much to be desired. Performance of its eighteen-year-old boys on selective service tests tells the sad tale of the failure to make bricks without straw.

School funding is a problem blacks and whites can form coalitions to solve. The problem and its attendant thrust is two-fold. First, state funding of schools is a necessity. Property-tax funding must be eliminated. Second, many states cannot adequately fund schools because of poverty and will need federal subsidies to assure a decent education for their children.

Several court cases have resulted in verdicts declaring property-tax school funding to be unconstitutional. The first and most widely publicized case was *Serrano* v. *Priest,* a California case. Suits have also been heard in Texas and Minnesota. All verdicts have been appealed, and a recent Supreme Court ruling stated that the plaintiffs had problems but that state legislatures and not the Supreme Court must solve the difficulties.

The problem of poor states has not been approached in these cases—a problem worthy of the attention of industry-government-school leadership. Federal contributions to education now comprise less than 10 percent of the total $50 billion or so spent each year. A 30 percent federal share is desirable. First, however, some way must be found to assure that states move to state financing of schools and that some do not reduce state funding when the new federal money arrives.

Groups must recognize the need to make sure that differentiated funding is assured poor children in the new scheme of things. Categorical federal programs such as Title I of the Elementary and Secondary Education Act of 1965 will need to be continued to assure this funding.

In a more perfect world, the State of Mississippi would assure a minimum of $500 of school funding to every child in the state. The federal government would assure another $500 for every child and yet another $500 for poor children. All children in Mississippi would receive a minimum of a $1,000 education, and poor children would receive a $1,500 education. In richer states, no federal subsidies would be required for all children, but the $500 for poor children would be necessary.

Many pitfalls are inherent in any plan to alter school funding.

In moving away from property taxes, states run the danger of placing an inordinate share of the tax burden on poor people by relying heavily on sales taxes to raise the needed revenue. The sales tax is a poor man's tax. Other sources must be found for school monies. Perhaps some method of devising a progressive sales tax can be developed. A combination sales and income tax plus full state tax levies upon industry and business might be the answer to equitable tax formulas.

Cheating is and will continue to be a problem where new school monies for needy children come into a community. The grasping and blatant misuse of Title I ESEA funds has been fully documented by the Washington Research Project, a foundation-supported group set up to monitor these and other federal expenditures for poor children.

Basically, what happened in many communities was a shifting of local funds from black schools to white schools and the use of Title I monies to replace the shifted funds. Where Title I was designed to provide one-half again as much money for the education of poor children in many communities, the children wound up with the same amount, while local monies were used to improve instruction and provide extras in the more affluent communities. In one Louisiana community, when Title I monies came to town a swimming pool materialized at the white high school. In the black schools the teacher-pupil ratio is the same as it has always been. Library books are still scarce and except for desultory attempts at a remedial-reading program, little has been done to help the children. Fortunately, school integration finally came to this community.

The Title I people recognize all of these inadequacies. Since 1970 USOE's Division of Compensatory Education has been led by Richard L. Fairley, an able black educator, and his capable staff. The problem is law and order at local and state levels. In spite of case after case of mismanagement and sometimes outright fraud, no one has been arrested and brought before the bar. Little wonder the belief is growing in America that courts and jails are for poor people. High on the agenda of business, government, and school administrators might be the securing of integrity in the management and use of the new monies.

Metropolitan Job Banks

This book was begun with a treatise on economic determinism in education. Again and again the author has pointed out thereafter that the strongest motivation for needy black youth to continue and do well in school is to see a former classmate land a good job. Conversely, the author has noted that the worst situation that can happen in this respect is to have large numbers of black high-school graduates roaming the streets looking for work.

Bad news must be reported in this area of youth unemployment, and the very first priority of business, government, and schools is to find a way to do something about it. In August of 1972 at a time of heavy pressure on black youth to stay in school, the U.S. Labor Department reported that 15.8 percent of all black young adults between the ages of eighteen and twenty-four were looking for work compared to only 8.1 percent of their white counterparts. Further, a higher percentage of black high-school graduates in this age group were unemployed than were white elementary-school dropouts (14.9 percent).[1]

Nothing can disrupt a strategy to improve the schooling of black youth more than this entirely untenable situation. Surely American ingenuity can solve this problem for such a small but important number of young people—the living, breathing carrots for the younger blacks in the lower grades. It is important that they succeed.

All told 3 million young blacks age eighteen to twenty-four are in this cohort. About 1.8 million are high-school graduates. Of this number, roughly 288,000 are out of work. Metropolitan job banks in the seventy-five or so metropolitan areas where most blacks live could solve this problem forthwith. Coupled with a stepped-up JOBS program, a job bank could wipe out all but the expected unemployment for job shifts (3 percent) in the black community.

A metropolitan job bank (hereafter called MJB) would serve black workers much as the Federal Reserve Bank serves banking or the Soil Bank serves big farmers or the Federal National Mortgage Association serves the suburbanite. The MJB would be a subsidy and become an addition to the $68 billion in subsidies of the federal government that annually flow to the well-connected and well-to-do in America.

The MJB would provide $5,000-a-year jobs to high-school graduates from needy families ($6,500 and under) who had spent three months looking in vain for work. The jobs would be with state, local, and federal agencies and with corporations and private firms contracting with these agencies. In the latter arrangements, contracts would provide for use of a certain number of MJB personnel. None of this procedure is new. German firms are required to hire up to 5 percent of their personnel in similar categories.

The MJB would deliver immediate placement. If a black June graduate walked into his neighborhood MJB office on September 1 and stated that he could not find work, he would look over computer print-outs of MJB jobs, select one, and report that afternoon. MJB job development experts would immediately begin to try to line up a good job either at home or through the labor mobility apparatus in another area.

MJB personnel would receive few raises and few promotions, for the facility is intended as a temporary, job entry, skills and job development operation. The young adult will hopefully move on to a $6,000 job with possibilities for advancement. His MJB job is returned to the bank.

Again, MJB is not a new idea. Full employment programs in many countries utilize this or similar approaches. Sweden and Germany are cases in point. Everybody benefits. The youngsters are working. The metropolitan area is getting work done. Taxes are being paid and the younger blacks know that a payoff comes with hard work and perseverance in school. One may deceive himself with rhetoric about love of knowledge and inner spirits as sustaining forces in school attendance and school completion, but he does not deceive others. Extrinsic rewards of jobs, incomes, and advancement, or the specter of hard times are the big guns in this process. Well-to-do and well-connected people can unlimber an overwhelming array of interim and final rewards for youth to stay on in school. Poor youth will need and benefit greatly from metropolitan job banks.

General Black Economic Development

School people must drop their reticence to point out the strong relationship between economic well-being and quality education and become strong advocates of economic development in the black community. The presence of nearly 300,000 unemployed black high-school graduates can make a mockery of the urgings of parents and teachers to finish high school. The devastating effects of economics on school achievement is even more revealing.

One has only to look at the British study *From Birth to Seven* to appreciate the impact that being poor has on schooling. This study will be examined in chapter 7. Business and government people must be led to understand that for every $1,000 in income added to the million black families mired in poverty, 30 percent is added to their children's performance in school.

Again, black economic development is proceeding on several fronts. All hands must understand the process, roll up their sleeves, and pitch in. Basically, black income is gained from the 15 percent of black workers who work in federal, state, or local government, 8 percent in the military, and about 20 percent in black-owned corporations, farms, or cooperatives. Ten percent of the black workers are unemployed, and the rest work for large and small corporations and businesses.

A better world would have black income derived from the following sources:

Government Workers	15%
Military	10%
Black Corporations, Firms, Farms and Cooperatives	40%
White Corporations and Firms'	32%
Unemployment Compensation	3%

A perfect world would have no unemployment compensation because there would be no unemployment; but in a free economy, job shifts account for a certain number of persons being "between jobs." Labor Department experts consider 3 percent an acceptable figure if the time between jobs can be kept at a minimum of fifteen weeks.

Energetic efforts on the part of the business community to spur development of black corporations, smaller firms, farms, and cooperatives seem imperative and should be high on the agenda. The Minority Enterprise Division of the U.S. Department of Commerce is doing yeoman's service in this area, and schools, colleges, governments, and corporations must do everything possible to cut young black corporations in on the action either through direct contracts or subcontracts. Higher education, for example, is a $28-billion business with many contracts for services, repairs, maintenance, and construction. Increased black participation means money in the family and brighter, better developed, and higher-reaching black children. The defense budget is $80 billion and the entire exchange of goods and services amounts to a trillion dollars. About $600 billion of this sum is generated by business.

A reachable and worthy goal for black business would be the generation of 40 percent of the $62 billion, which would be an equitable black share in this operation. This sum—$25 billion—would require 5,000 black firms averaging $2 million in sales each year, another 5,000 averaging $500,000, and a gaggle of 40,000 or so firms, farms, cooperatives and "mom and pop" stores averaging $300,000 and less. Such an operation would provide jobs for 3.6 million black workers. This approach seems to be a large order but there are over 5 million businesses in America and 3 million farms. Everybody is making and selling something. The black expansion described above would require only about 50,000 active participants and there are plenty of those around. Corporations such as Parks Sausage and Johnson Publications already gross in top figures. Thirty-five black millionaires live in this country—many operating large land holdings in the South. Some cooperatives are operating in the top range. American corporations, governments, and schools must cut these innovators in for a bigger share of the action and do business with blacks.

Perfecting School and College Programs

Nothing is so effective in developing the type of school programs needed in communities as a good business-industry-government-school working relationship. If the school boards and state and national advisory bodies and interest groups can constantly ask questions about what is needed and what is working, one does not have much to worry about where momentum in the education of black Americans is concerned. This type of pragmatic to-hell-with-ideology approach will cut through the confusion, vested interests, tunnel vision, and general ossification that plagues monopolistic enterprises such as schools and virtually precludes the development of meaningful programs. A national priority list for such a coalition might look as follows:

1. 100,000 new classrooms for 3 million black children now locked into school ruins
2. Cradle schools for 150,000 black infants annually (30 percent of total born)
3. Year-round preschool programs for 350,000 black children at ages three and four (700,000 children total)
4. 750,000 black high-school youth in work-study programs, about one-third of the high-school cohorts
5. 1.2 million black children and youth engaged in some activity designed to challenge gifted children, about 20 percent of the 6 million enrolled
6. 1.4 million black youth in college-bound curricula
7. 25,000 black youth in preparatory schools operated by colleges, civic groups, and the military
8. Scholarship aid based on need and awarded on an automatic, no-red-tape basis for 600,000 black college students, about three-fourths of the 800,000 that should be enrolled
9. A qualified teacher free of racism in every classroom
10. Fully integrated administrative staffs
11. "Job-getting" technical education
12. Revamped special education

13. A new breed of guidance counselors
14. A full range of continuation education
15. An overhaul of the testing apparatus
16. Control and reduction of research on black children
17. A new breed of metropolitan colleges
18. A constant strengthening of black colleges and universities
19. Expansion of federal scholarships for black graduate and professional study
20. Metropolitan job banks for 300,000 youth in 75 major metropolitan areas

Many challenges exist to occupy the social energies of the business-government-school partnership. Further, all programs outlined *deliver*—none are the extensions of the neuroses of a professor. Coupled with the economic dynamism discussed earlier, the programs will push a larger number of blacks into the mainstream. The combined dynamics will be synergistic.

Many of these programs have been analyzed but price tags have not been affixed. Others, such as research in the black community, will be discussed. The price list includes capital expenditures such as new classrooms and ongoing annual expenditures such as cradle schools:

1. 100,000 Classrooms	$ 4.5	billion
2. Cradle Schools	$ 1.0	billion
3. Preschools	$ 2.0	bililon
4. Gifted Programs	$ 1.0	billion
5. Preparatory Schools	$ 0.2	billion
6. Collgee Scholarships	$ 1.0	billion
7. Graduate Fellowships	$ 0.5	billion
8. New Metropolitan Colleges (Plants)	$ 1.8	billion
9. Strengthening Black Colleges and New Metropolitan Colleges	$ 1.0	billion
10. Metropolitan Job Banks	$ 1.5	billion
Total	$14.5	billion
Capital Expenditure	$ 7.0	billion
Annual Current Fund Expenditure	$ 7.5	billion

A capital expenditure of $7 billion and an annual current fund outlay of $7.5 billion, coupled with increased economic improvements will be necessary for such a program as estimated in this analysis. Some preschool programs are already operating, as are some scholarship programs. If these programs are folded into the budget, new money for annual operations would be slightly less than $7 billion.

Two thorny problems emerge. One problem has to do with the replacement of decrepit school plants in, say, the inner cities with 100,000 new classrooms. All federal school programs to date have prohibited building and rightfully so. A federal program similar to the W.P.A. would get this job done, get many of the 800,000 unemployed black workers back on the job, and provide contracts for the new black building cooperatives. A quasi-public corporation named, say, Public Works Corporation (PWC), similar to the Federal National Mortgage Corporation, might be the vehicle for getting this done. PWC would move into a city, sit down with a school administration, negotiate for a local share of 25 percent of building costs, decide on sites and number of classrooms, contract with as many black builders as possible, build the schools, give the keys to the superintendent, and leave.

PWC would operate in no more than fifteen communities at any given time, thereby enabling the executives to assure quality and efficiency in their operations. In five years PWC would have built its classrooms in the seventy-five metropolitan areas where most blacks live and could move into the countryside. By contrast, the average school building project takes five years, from planning, to floating the bond issue (failure rates now 60 percent), to letting bids, to actual construction, to final turning over of keys.

Although the quasi-public corporation and the local cost share is new, this concept is not. The building housing this writer's office was built under W.P.A. aegis during the Depression. Some of the better built local, state, and federal buildings came into being via this route.

The other thorny problem has to do with improving the salary schedules at black colleges through federal funding. This improvement is entirely necessary if black colleges are going to keep pace and serve the black community as they should.

The government is now engaged in a drive to assure black colleges a greater share of the research money. In the land-grant area, for example, this has been an acute problem. At this writing, land-grant funds have been eliminated from the federal budget, but historically seventeen or so land-grant black colleges are included in the annual pleas to Congress for funds. Almost none of this money is awarded to them as research funds. Their students and faculties have been exploited as statistics for increasing appropriations to white colleges.

The Title III program of the Higher Education Act of 1965 is spending about $50 million annually to help developing colleges. The average black college receives about $300,000 annually for strengthening instructional programs. Some sort of project is required and an annual proposal must be acted on.

The single biggest problem of black colleges is competing in a national instead of regional marketplace for good faculty. Black state colleges match white state colleges in their regions. Few black universities match white university salaries on a national scale, however, and private black colleges do not match private white colleges in the regions. Further, the South, where most black colleges are located, generally pays lower salaries than other regions. This economic fact of life further complicates things. In fairness, one must note that Southern living costs are lower and the entire economy is geared to a slower pace.

A black public university representative at a hiring table at the Modern Language Association, for example, will find himself able to pay only 85 percent of what his white neighboring university can pay. The white university, in turn, can pay only 90 percent of what a comparable Northern university can pay. The black university is simply not in a national competitive position. Hosts of strong, able professors teach at black colleges and universities. But not for money. These teachers, black and white, are subsidizing American higher education through their dedication.

A government policy of assuring class A scales as defined

by the American Association of University Professors (AAUP) for 70 percent of the black colleges and universities and an AA ranking for ten first-class universities would bring enormous changes to these schools and tremendous benefits to the entire American community. The subsidy, once decided upon, should be as automatic as the budget for the land-grant activities or any of the other encrusted programs. Blacks can boast five exceptionally strong black universities and two good medical schools. Ten strong universities each with a full complement of medicine and law and business schools plus 115 or so colleges able to compete for faculty on a national scale would spin the wheels of progress. The FSS (Federal Salary Supplement) may be the key.

Desegregating Administrative Ranks

Quality education for black Americans will depend heavily on the degree to which black administrators can move into leadership positions at all levels. Some of the most able educators in the country are black. The California and Michigan systems have been led by black state superintendents (Wilson Riles took the reins in California in 1970 and John Porter in Michigan one year later). Universities in Massachusetts, Michigan, and California have black presidents. Several large school districts have black superintendents, including Oakland, Baltimore, Atlanta, and Wilmington. However, education has a long history of bigotry to live down and a long way to go before minorities have complete access to administrative slots.

Thirty years ago all superintendents were white except in a few all-black towns in the South and most principals were white except in Southern dual systems. White professors of education trained these administrators. Historically, gentlemen's agreements were reached that no black administrators would be trained. Phi Delta Kappa, the school leadership fraternity, had a white-only membership clause.

In 1973, thirty or so Northern city school systems had heavy black enrollments and countless Southern districts had similar enrollments. These students and parents want and need black administrators in top positions. Mollifying rhetoric that seeks to explain away a history of bigotry and efforts to continue this sad state of affairs in the face of increasingly vigorous efforts to halt it will create chaos.

The special case of firing, demotion, or silent firing of administrators in Southern schools needs to be dealt with. Virginia is a case in point. This state had some of the most able black high-school principals in the country and one of the more productive school systems for blacks although it was segregated. Scientists, physicians, the best civil-rights lawyers, and the only black admiral were produced in these schools. The ranks of black high-school principals have dwindled from a high of 107 in 1953 to 17 in 1972. Many black principals have been replaced by less able whites. Both blacks and whites in these schools are getting less education because of this disadvantage.

No mystery surrounds how to remedy this situation. The solution is simple: Hire black administrators. The solution for biased schools of education is simple: Train black administrators or remit that portion of the appropriations for the units that would have gone into this sort of training. The solution for Southern districts is simple: Hire black administrators almost exclusively for vacated slots until a better situation has been created. Develop smaller multiple high-school units of one thousand to twelve hundred students. Assign black administrators. Some of the larger units are inefficient and harm students anyway.

The industry-government-school partnership has a big role to play in this process. Simply put, the complex asserts pressure. The taxpayers simply cannot spend $7 billion of the regular school budgets and $7.5 billion of a new federal program to improve the schooling of black children and youth and have this money squandered because some people want to practice discrimination in the executive suite. The country is making this effort in its own self-interest and is counting on the schools to prepare blacks for full participation in the economy and civic life of the country. Bigots in the executive suite are completely expendable in this context.

In a more perfect world, every heavily black school district would have black administrators in top slots from time to time and every district enrolling blacks would have these people on a less frequent basis. State departments of education and the U.S. Office of Education would follow suit. All departments of administration at teacher-training colleges would be integrated, as would all guilds, unions, fraternities, and sororities serving this establishment. These improvements must be done if all other pieces in the puzzle are to fit into place.

A New Testing Apparatus

A serious drive is presently underway to reform the testing apparatus in the schools. The business-government-school partnership must join forces to assure success. The partnership is important because all three members have stakes in testing. All will profit in some way in eliminating tests that are counterproductive to quality education for black children and youth from depressed areas.

The previous discussion stresses the necessity of showing how moving away from IQ tests in schools with poor black children is essential, how gifted black children fail to be identified because of bad testing, how well-meaning researchers serve up biased data for racist degenerates to twist and serve their purposes, how exact measures of what children are able to perform after instruction are not available.

One should mention how vested interests in business and schools perpetuate these ills, or how vested interests plus a certain ineptness on the part of federal government officials join forces to assure disaster in this area.

First, standardized school testing is big business in America. All of the 3 million kindergarten children receive at least two tests a year. The 33.2 million elementary students receive at least one test and the 14.5 million high-school students might average two or more. In addition, tests are used to measure the results of special projects and programs and for data of graduate students writing theses.

The Educational Testing Service, which handles much of the high-school testing, grossed $28.5 million in 1971. American College Testing, a smaller firm that operates in the Midwest, grossed $7 million. Psychological Corporation, which publishes many instruments used in New York and other districts, grossed $7 million. One can go on but the point is clear. Testing means jobs and money. A Reuters study of testing in America pegged the gross sales of test and test services at $300 million annually. Business has not given special attention to the needs of minorities in testing because such attention would not be profitable. The testing corporations will turn their attention to these needs when making a profit becomes the case.

School administrators and teachers usually use tests that corporation salesmen from the six large companies in this field manage to convince them are desirable and trendy. Their test experts have usually been trained in colleges where professors sometimes advise these corporations and in any case tout certain tests. Because of a lack of awareness, educators rarely get pressure from parents and community groups on the counterproductivity of the apparatus. Ironically, community pressure is directed toward having the children do better on the bad measures.

Federal bureaucrats unwittingly contribute to the problem by requiring evaluation by tests for their myriad programs and by providing funds for the purchase of tests. Since 1957 when the National Defense Education Act was passed, some $12–14 million in federal funds has been available for improvement of guidance programs in schools. Much of this money, now distributed under Title III of the Elementary and Secondary Education Act of 1965, goes for testing. Further, the $2-billion Title I and similar programs stipulate "hard" evaluation data and set aside 5 percent of the funding for this operation—which translates into more tests.

The leadership initiative must come from the federal government. Much of the swollen sales of the test corporations come from federal appropriations. Prior to 1957, many schools had *no* tests. In trimming the budget such "frills" were usually the first to go. Interestingly, many poor children got a better education in the no-test era. The writer posed this question to members of a Congressional committee, none of whom could remember receiving a single test. Some wondered out loud if they would have made it to the Congress—or into the school graduation procession—if the testing apparatus had been arrayed against them as ferociously as it works against some children today.

If the Offices of Education and Child Development stipulated the use of improved measures in their guidelines on evaluation and pointed out that use of old culturally biased, normative-based testing is unacceptable, reform would be swift.

The interests of teachers and school administrators in test reform can also play a big role in this reform. The National Education Association passed a resolution calling for a moratorium on testing for everyone at its annual conference in February, 1972. A resolution calling for reforms in testing of *all* children was passed by the National Association of Elementary School Principals at its June, 1972, meeting. The interest exists and is growing. Thirty-two thousand psychologists work in America, but two million teachers and administrators are part of the school system. The tail is wagging the dog. Blacks are in the fortunate position of being able to join forces with whites on a project of mutual interest. The problem now is picking a direction in which to move. The criterion-referenced tests mentioned earlier might hold promise. These tests will be examined more closely at this juncture.

An unusual amount of interest and activity surrounds criterion-referenced test (CRT) measurement. The subject occupied a major portion of the energies of the recent conference of the American Educational Research Association. Several large test corporations have placed CRTs on the market, and almost every new teaching system utilizes CRT measurement for unit and course evaluation. In a survey of twenty-four bellwether school systems conducted by the National Leadership Institute in Teacher Education, sixteen were using criterion tests or had plans to use them the next year.[2]

CRT measurement is a logical development stemming from desires of psychometrists to perfect their measurement techniques in a more sophisticated way than previously afforded by normative-based testing. More important, perhaps, has been the response by test publishers to the demands of teachers and administrators for accurate, valid instruments to measure outcomes of individualized instruction. Remarkable strides are being made toward the individualization of the curriculum in American schools, and a form of measurement to measure student progress is the CRT.

How do criterion tests differ from normative-based tests? What advantages do they offer teachers and children?

Criterion-referenced tests measure student progress toward explicit objectives as defined by the school enterprise. The tests measure the degree of mastery of material taught and learned in a specific time frame. The tests have a high degree of individual relevance and validity; the major intent is to measure individual progress and identify needed additional experiences to assure mastery of instructional objectives. These measurements afford teachers and children the opportunity to focus on mastery of material that enables them to progress to a higher level of study and that will eventually enable them to function properly and easily in American society.

Normative-based tests (NBT) serve more of a sorting function in the schools. These tests measure children in relation to each other rather than in an individualized manner. Measurement of instructional objectives is often difficult with NBT measurement, as the tests are keyed to comparisons of all children tested to the norm group on which the NBT was standardized. Item tap, objectives, and material priorities all pose problems for the teacher in attempting to individualize instruction for her class while at the same time making sure that the children make a good showing on the normative-based test that will be administered at the end of the school term. A poor showing on what has been defined as an essential corpus by commercial test publishers can have an adverse effect on the teacher's career. A poor showing by a school can affect both teachers and administrators. School administrators are becoming concerned about these effects. A widely publicized resolution at the 1972 convention of the National Association of Elementary School Principals called for reforms in the test syndrome in the schools. The president of this group noted that the schools were being inundated with tests and that undue pressures and strains were being placed on the children. He noted that tests used for diagnostic and individualized instruction were excellent and should be the trend of the future.

Criterion-referenced testing has both advantages and disadvantages. The latter to a large extent involves technical difficulties, which psychometrists can be expected to overcome in a matter of time. In summary, some advantages of criterion-referenced testing are:

1. Direct interpretation of progress in terms of specified behavioral objectives.
2. Facilitation of individualized instruction.
3. Elimination of a situation where half of the American schoolchildren must always be below the median. In normative-based testing, half of the children must always "lose." If all children were raised to or above the median, the tests would be made harder and the time shortened.
4. Many CR tests are short summative tests that enable teachers to check on student progress at regular intervals.
5. Eliminates pressures on teachers to "teach to the test" in order to have children make a good showing.
6. Enables teachers to compile a comprehensive record of the child's development. Further instruction can be pegged at clearly identified points.

Some disadvantages of criterion-referenced testing are:

1. Reporting systems will vary and must be interpreted for children moving into new districts.
2. Further work on construct validation must be done.
3. Comparisons of performance of school districts are not readily available.
4. Materials for teaching toward specified objectives must *always* be available if tests are to be valid.

Criterion tests are valuable for all children and serve teachers well as instruments and tools of instruction. These tests offer teachers a special tool where minority children are concerned, especially those mired in poverty for whom direct, high-impact instruction is being offered.

Standardized tests measure the abilities and achievements of middle-class minority children almost as well as they measure these attributes for middle-class majority children. These tests are not accurate for poor minority children, however. As noted in chapter 2, Jane Mercer of the University of California has completed one of the most revealing studies of this dynamic. Mercer found a very high relationship between similarities in minority-majority life-styles and scores on standardized tests. Black children in Mercer's study averaged 100 on IQ tests, for example, if family life-styles rated 100 each on five life-style descriptors taken from white middle-class communities. Children from families rated lower on these scales had lower scores. Similar findings were made for other minority groups in Mercer's study.[3]

A testing program utilizing CRTs as basic instruments enables teachers and administrators to avoid the hazards inherent in applications of normative-based tests to poor minority children. A teacher may have done a herculean job of working with a group of poor children over the year. She is pleased with the job she has done, and the children are happy with their growth and look forward to continued development. Every indication points to their mastering the curriculum with a little extra work and time. Because of the flaws in the normative-based tests, however, this teacher might well be criticized instead of praised for her efforts. This criticism may come from her supervisors, newspaper writers who have limited knowledge of testing, or concerned community groups who also have not considered all of the ramifications involved.

In an improved situation, utilizing CRTs, the teacher would administer a placement or formative test using material to be mastered as criteria and teach the children for a year. Over this period, she would have administered many summative tests indicating mastery of the units and skills she set out to teach during the year. A final comprehensive summative test might be given. The children would end the year with comprehensive, explicit records with this system. The CRT-based system would indicate what they set out to learn, what they had learned, and the point at which learning should begin in the next school year. In normative-based testing, only an age-grade score is recorded, indicating that the children had matched, exceeded, or failed to match the performance of a norm group of children on whatever items the commercial test publisher placed in the test.

All of the large test publishers have marketed at least one criterion-referenced test. The *California Prescriptive Reading and Arithmetic Inventories* have been marketed by the California Test Bureau, which is now a subsidiary of McGraw-Hill Book Company. Random House publishers have developed *Criterion Reading Tests* and Psychological Corporation, the *Boehm Test of Basic Concepts*. Science Research Associates publish *Diagnosis: An Instructional Aid.*

Some excellent tests are being developed by state and local schools. The Clark County, Nevada, schools have CRTs for language arts, science, social studies, and physical education, and the Atlanta school system has developed a CRT for its Comprehensive Instructional Program.

Most of the new instructional systems use CRTs. Such reading and arithmetic programs as Individually Prescribed Instruction, DISTAR, and the new Ginn Southwestern Laboratories Program are good examples.

An example of the specificity and comprehensiveness of CRT measurement and its usefulness to the teacher might be the California Prescriptive Reading Inventory. PRI includes a "diagnostic map" for each student showing which specific objectives have or have not been mastered. A study guide refers teacher and child to material valuable in reaching these objectives; a class "diagnostic map" is available and a class grouping report to facilitate the forming of groups is included.

Again, a vital amount of interest and resources is currently directed toward development of measurement systems utilizing criterion-referenced tests. CRT measurement is an effort to perfect further measurement techniques begun some sixty-five years ago and refined constantly over the years. CRT measurement is also a response to the needs for new tests to fit the rapid individualization of instruction that schools are pressing.

CRT measurement has great value for all children and enables teachers and administrators to do a better job of measurement and reporting in schools with children from poor minority families.

Most major test publishers have marketed criterion-referenced tests and more are on the way. State and local school agencies are also developing tests. More refined CRTs can be expected in the future as all hands gain experience and expertise in this area.

Again, interest and urging on the part of the biggest financial supporter of testing programs, the federal government, plus increased awareness and activity on the part of school teachers and administrators—their guilds and their communities—will make the elimination of test flaws that hamper the full development of both black *and* white children profitable for business. Again, blacks will not have to carry this load alone. Eliminating faulty tests affects all schoolchildren. Blacks will find assistance in the white community in a drive for reform.

Research Reforms

A final part of the agenda for the business-government-school partnership is a look at the research situation in relation to the black community. The simple fact is, first, that the black community is being overstudied, and second, that a huge amount of this research is inaccurate.

One might note from the outset that, moral consideration aside, quality education is not possible if an inordinate number of studies are underway in a school. Further, large numbers of black parents and children are disaffected by research abuses. This disaffection has the triple impact of rendering invalid an even greater number of studies, of feeding an even larger amount of inaccurate information to the sensationalist media, and of angering an ever larger number of black parents and communities when they read the "news."

Many black and white parents feel that research on the poorer elements of both blacks and whites has come dangerously close to some of the things that went on in Hitler's Germany. In those sad years, Nazis herded their guinea pigs into concentration camps to test ghoulish theories that might enable Deutschlanders to live a happier life. Americans use welfare rolls to make groups submit to experimentation. Uncooperative subjects become disenrolled welfare recipients. In 1972, there was a general uproar when the news was released about a forty-year study conducted by the U.S. Public Health Service to determine if a certain venereal disease would shorten a man's life. To see if life were shortened by this disease, a total of four hundred afflicted persons for forty years were denied treatment or knowledge of their affliction. All of the afflicted were poor blacks from rural Alabama.

In the name of psychological research, poor children are sometimes denied access to quality tried-and-true instruction. Poor students are often recipients of an instructional program that has doubtful value but that is tested for its usefulness to the researchers. The latter phrase *usefulness to the researcher* is the key to the dilemma. The problem is bound up in the changing times and the changing role of research in our colleges and universities. In the old days, researchers were useful to the black community. Today, the black community, in many cases, is useful to researchers. As a result of this changing dynamic, demand has risen from the black community for white researchers to remove themselves forthwith. A fall, 1973 issue of the *Journal of Social Issues* takes up this question. Also as a protest, at least in part, of research abuse in the black community, one recognizes a proliferation of black guilds and a pulling away from the leadership of the major groups serving these professions. A dynamic National Association of Black Psychologists and a National Association of Black Social Workers have now emerged. Black and white membership in the old Association for the Study of Negro Life and History is growing. A new Afro-American Teachers Association has arrived on the scene. Part of this pulling away has the same roots as the actions of Richard Allen in leading black Methodists from the balconies and basements of Philadelphia churches. Much of the alienation has to do with a sickening disgust at exploitation of blacks at the hands of white researchers and the increase in the use of research to direct surreptitious and/or subliminal racism at the black community.

What went wrong? Where are the beautiful white researchers like Franz Boas, Gunnar Myrdal, or Otto Klineberg? Some such researchers are still around, but increasingly they are pale voices bleating in the wilderness, smothered by avalanches of large university teams and federal dollars.

Several dynamics conspired to produce this situation. First, a huge increase in college faculty and in the number of Ph.D. graduates has taken place in the large universities seeking to become known as research-oriented schools. College faculties have grown from 250,000 or so in 1950 to nearly 700,000 full-time and part-time teachers. The number of large research-oriented schools has grown from less than fifty to more than two hundred. At least twice this number are trying hard to break into research-oriented status. Ph.D. production has sky-rocketed from 9,000 to 32,000 per year. An annual output of 50,000 is projected for the next ten years, although the unemployment rate is high. Presently, about 6,000 education and 1,800 psychology doctorates are graduated annually.

Research abuse is easy to understand in such a context. All of the graduate students must do research for their dissertations. All of the young faculty must present research outputs for their promotions. The larger universities must be able to point to "significant ongoing research." The aspirants for research-oriented status must present twice as much. Add to this vortex a federal government interested in advancing the cause of quality schooling for minorities and earmarking 5 to 10 percent of its appropriations for research in this cause. Blacks become grist for the government-university research mills.

The new researcher could often care less about the validity of his instruments. The dissertation must be written. The tenure and promotions committee must be convinced of research output. "Hot media" reporters want to know if he is working on something worthy of a news wire release. At last count, for example, some seven hundred evaluations of Head Start had been presented.

The new researcher is often a blatant racist and, like the

antiblack minister who went mad after being swept along to the Selma March with a delegation from his church, may hate blacks. Nevertheless, if he wants to produce, he is chained to the enterprise. His research designs and methods of reporting findings reflect this fevered state. Blacks and other minorities are mangled in the process.

Also thriving is the surreptitious racist who in a time of increased federal funds to assist minorities finds concealment of his racism beneficial. He sometimes piously parades as a man of good will in order to garner the benefits of the helping professions. Again, racism shines through in his designs and presentations of findings.

Also prevalent is the subliminal racist's maneuvering at the trough. This man is convinced of his good intentions and rude awakenings to his true inner feelings often come as a devastating blow. Abe Fortas in a *New York Times* Op-Ed article has described this dynamic well.[4] Fortas notes that blacks and their white allies must gird for an increase in this kind of racism. Fortas describes his life as a child in the Mississippi Delta and the bigotry directed against Catholics, Jews, and blacks. He notes that historically bigotry is directed most intensely against a group on the rise, that Jews and Catholics had to stand against virulent bigotry on their way up the ladder, and that blacks can understand the new subliminal racism in this way. Fortas contends the reaction is frightened and sometimes envious. People fear the competition of a vigorous, dedicated race and of their different ways of doing things. The subliminal racist may flee the city because of this fear, feel uneasy on city streets because of the black presence, worry about blacks taking his job or becoming a large minority in his new community. Exasperated in myriad ways by a black presence, he vents this exasperation in the designing and reporting of his research.

The patterns of racist research are easy to spot. Invalid tests are used and results are reported without qualifications. White middle-class children are matched with lower-class black children. The factor of bigotry and discrimination is never discussed. Whites outstripping blacks are heralded. Blacks outstripping whites are ignored. Middle-class blacks are ignored and upper-class blacks cannot be recognized to exist.

A variation on this theme involves whites who are not racists but who suffer from the missionary-racist syndrome. In this syndrome, the researcher was drawn to the helping professions as a means of relieving self-contempt. This affliction may have befallen him for a variety of reasons that are not important in this discussion. Importantly, the missionary-racist must help someone in order to feel better about himself. Important, then, to his mental health is the necessity that blacks fail so they will continue to need his help. Researchers caught up in the missionary-racist syndrome become alarmed at the upward surge of blacks and make every effort to discredit any progress, pick flaws in any effective program, and set new goals when blacks have reached the last plateau he set. Upon hearing reports that blacks bought 700,000 homes in new housing developments, both the missionary-racist and the subliminal racist will be quick to note that much of this movement is simply a spreading of city boundaries. A new term *inner suburbs* is created, and blacks can still have racism directed at them from the latter and serve to help the self-concept of the former.

As in the drive for test reform, the federal government is going to have to take a leadership role in making research once again a part of the solution instead of part of the problem. Congressional hearings might look into this dynamic. More writing similar to the Society for the Psychological Study of Social Issues in their *Journal of Social Issues* would help. Beneficial, too, would be discussion of this problem at national meetings of the guilds.

Deans, trustee boards, and presidents must also exercise leadership. Mustering respect for educational leaders who posture about the country trumpeting high-sounding rhetoric while their faculties are engaged in a pitiful scramble to exploit oppressed minorities for survival as members of their faculties is difficult.

Mustering respect for a commissioner of education or an assistant secretary of education or a Secretary of Health, Education, and Welfare who will sign forms awarding bad research projects, or for a director of the new National Institute of Education if his $200 million for research on learning is not directed in such a way as to avoid racism in research would be difficult.

The latter point cannot be overemphasized. Congress has authorized the National Institute of Education and appropriated funds for its operation. The direction this new agency takes will be crucial. Every effort must be made in its shaping years to have the agency become a force for more accurate instruments, more accurate designs, and more accurate reporting of research findings. The business-government-school partnership can play a powerful role in bringing about these goals. Research must once again become a part of the solution.

Notes for Chapter 6

[1] The *New York Times,* August 13, 1972, p. 35.

[2] "Criterion-Referenced Tests: Incidence of Use in Selected School Districts," Mimeographed. National Leadership Institute Teacher Education, University of Connecticut.

[3] Jane Mercer, "Socio-Cultural Factors in School Testing of Minorities," (Paper presented at the February, 1972 Human Relations Conference of the National Education Association, Washington, D.C.).

[4] The *New York Times,* July 18, 1972, p. 33.

CHAPTER 7

Agenda for the Black Community

THIS book began by noting the tremendous surge ahead of blacks in the field of education. The author noted possibilites of an 80 percent high-school graduation rate by 1980. Also, possibilities of significant rises in college-bound black youth were noted. The relationship between economics and education was stressed and economic gains of blacks assessed. New horizons were discussed and goals of 100 percent high-school graduation by 1999 (regular or GED diploma) were outlined. College enrollment based on labor-market demands for college-trained workers was mentioned. The need to generate steep rises in physicians, lawyers, and academic doctorates was stressed, and the importance of scholarship support to get these increases was highlighted.

Problem areas were analyzed throughout the treatise, including school testing apparatus that deny access of many black children to quality education and proceed to measure their progress as if they had access to this schooling. Also, the inordinate relegation of black children to retarded classes and vocational-education programs, and failures and sometimes racism in the guidance and executive suites of the educational establishment at local, state, and federal levels were analyzed. The need for new types of metropolitan colleges and the need for black youth and adults to make more effective use of continuing education were analyzed. The responsibilities of a business-government-school partnership were enumerated and a price tag affixed to various components of the drive.

Throughout this discussion the agenda for the black community has been referred to mainly in reference to problem areas requiring community concern and action. More important, perhaps, is the role of the black community in maintaining the vigor and joie de vivre in this drive. If the premonitions of this writer are correct, the intensity of the drive will increase with more black derring-do in economic areas, more startling cooperative developments, and a general fashioning of new types of continuing and higher education. A general freeing of elementary and high schools with more pluralism in programs will be the result of efforts to reach children mired in poverty.

Much of this agenda for the black community will parallel that of the business-government-school partnership in some cases. The agenda might well center around community and political action designed to achieve the following:

1. Cradle school slots for that 30 percent of black children born into poverty each year, about 150,000 (300,000 for two-year programs)
2. Preschool slots for 700,000 black three-to-four-year-olds (200,000 are already enrolled)
3. High-impact programs in every classroom where such programs are needed
4. Work-study slots for 750,000 high-school youth
5. Enrollment of 1.2 million gifted black children in special programs
6. Enrollment of 1.4 million black high-school youth in college-bound curricula
7. Enrollment of 25,000 black youth in preparatory schools
8. Automatic full scholarships for 600,000 black college students
9. A qualified teacher free of racism in every classroom
10. Top black leadership in local, state, and federal school units
11. Quality technical and special education
12. Expansion of continuing education
13. New metropolitan colleges
14. More federal and state support for black colleges

15. More federal scholarships for black enrollees in medical and law schools
16. Elimination of counterproductive tests
17. Elimination of counterproductive research
18. Metropolitan job banks for 300,000 black high-school graduates

In some instances, the black community will plow new ground. Such pioneering efforts might include the following:

1. Modifications of black demography to assure better resources for the development of black children and youth
2. Expansion of the cooperatives movement
3. Generation of added black entrepreneurs and corporations
4. Generation of added aspirants for medical, legal, and Ph.D. training
5. Expansion of research on the mental processes of white racists of all persuasions—blatant, surreptitious, subliminal, and missionary; expanded dissemination of results of this research
6. Expanded research on black history and black culture and expanded dissemination of these findings
7. Development of five additional major black universities with full ranges of medicine, law, and business offerings
8. Expanded community control and community involvement to assure that schools serve and not rule black communities
9. Community programs for gifted chidren
10. Expanded contacts and cultural exchanges with African schools and universities

Nearly a thirty-year span remains in which to do the work that must be done. Further, much of the joie de vivre of the present and upcoming generation of blacks will derive from getting this job done. Nothing is so rewarding and unifying to a people as cooperative endeavors around which to rally. In a way, blacks might feel blessed in a time of rootlessness and search for purpose that plagues many American communities.

Now for an analysis of aspects of the agenda that demand careful attention by the black community.

Access to Quality Education

The black agenda might well begin with the guarantee of access to quality education. In fact, this drive has been under way for years. What the community must concern itself with is the removal of school practices that are counterproductive and deny black children access to the very best instruction in schools and, in some cases, to certain school programs.

A black community girding for work on its agenda might begin with the problem of school testing for needy children. As noted earlier, school tests are not accurate for needy black children and hurt them in many ways. The tests relegate many to classes for the retarded where the instruction is vapid and the children are stigmatized by labels. Faulty tests give a false impression to teachers of the capabilities of needy children and cause teachers to slow the pace of instruction and convey to the children in myriad ways a mirror image of inadequacies and truncated potential. These tests must be eliminated and the newer, more advanced locator-criterion measures must replace them. Community and political action is indicated.

Black community groups might simply petition school boards for reform as has been done in many cases. Consultants from the National Association of Black Psychologists might be retained to offer guidance in these efforts. The home office of this group is the University of California at Riverside. Its president, Dr. Reginald Jones, took office in 1971. Black psychologists work in most of the colleges and universities in the nation and many work in school systems and hospitals. Others have private practices and still others work as industrial psychologists with corporations. Little difficulty would be experienced by black community groups in availing themselves of expert assistance in an effort to bring about a change in their school's testing machinery. Many white psychologists recognize these problems and will be happy to assist. In fact, many white psychologists hold membership in the National Association of Black Psychologists, as do many blacks hold membership in the white American Psychological Association.

If petitions to school boards fail, a second plan is a suit in local or federal district courts to enjoin the school board to cease and desist in practices denying equal access to school offerings by the schools.

An increase in these suits has been witnessed over the past year or so. The National Leadership Institute in Teacher Education identified eighteen class-action suits in 1972 involving a wide variety of test abuses.[1] Figure 15 contains a listing of these cases. They range from a case in Lancaster, Pennsylvania, where schools refused to educate children scoring beneath a certain level on tests, to a suit against a California superintendent of schools for inappropriate classification and retarded class placement of children. Many suits were filed against Southern systems and many of the Western suits involve Spanish-American children.

Class-action suits filed in most states enrolling large numbers of black children will serve to shape school policy. Black community groups must still examine local school practices and petition the board when these practices are in violation of state law and court rulings. A petition in the wake of a court ruling will usually bring results. Black state legislators might also follow the lead of California's black and brown (Spanish) state assembly members and sponsor legislation designed to get at educational inequality. In a span of two years, California legislators have sponsored more than five pieces of education-related legislation. The contents of the bills are instructive and tell the black community as plainly as anything what sorts of problems they must deal with in alleviating problems in the schools.

A brown and black group of legislators sponsored a bill designed to prohibit schools from testing children who had not been in America for two years.[2] Blacks all over America could rally support from immigrant groups for such a piece of legislation. This testing has probably hampered the schooling of more immigrant children than any other aspect of school practices. This bill might be modified to read "in the country

FIGURE 15
COURT CASES INVOLVING STANDARDIZED TESTS

Locale	Plaintiff	Defendant	Organization Assisting Plaintiff	Grievance
Boston, Mass.	Association for Mentally Ill Children	Greenblatt	Boston Legal Assistance Project	Improper classification of various categories of children
Washington, D.C.	Mills	D.C. Board of Education	National Legal Aid Defenders Association National Law Office	Failure to educate classes of handicapped and intractable children
Lancaster-Lebanon, Pa. (Eastern District)	Pennsylvania Association for Retarded Children	Kurzman	None	Failure to educate school-age children who score below a specified mental age on standardized tests
New Orleans, La.	Lebanks	Spears	New Orleans Legal Aid Commission	Exclusion of retarded children
Tempe, Ariz.	Guadalupe Organization	Tempe Elementary School District #3	Maricopa County Legal Services	Tracking of Spanish-speaking children on basis of results on English language tests
Boston, Mass.	Massachusetts Commission Against Discrimination	Boston School Committee	Boston Legal Assistance Project	Challenge on behalf of poor and minority children to the admission standards and procedures to Boston's elite schools

Location	Case	Defendant	Plaintiff	Issue
Monterey County, Calif.	Diana	California State Board of Education	California Rural Legal Assistance Program	Placement of children in mentally retarded classes on basis of IQ tests given in English to Spanish-speaking children
San Diego, Calif.	Covarrubias	San Diego Unified School District	California Rural Legal Assistance Program	Disproportionate placement of black and non-English-speaking children in mentally retarded classes on basis of biased test scores
San Francisco, Calif.	Larry P.	Riles	California Rural Legal Assistance Program; San Francisco Neighborhood Legal Assistance Foundation; NAACP Legal Defense Fund	Inappropriate classification and placement in classes for mentally retarded (black children)
Pasadena, Calif.	Spangler	Pasadena City Board of Education	Justice Department	Interclass grouping based upon discriminatory tests violated the rights of minority children
Jackson, La.	Johnson	Jackson Parish School Board	Justice Department	Elimination of segregated classes within "desegregated" schools; classes assigned by tests
Bossier, La.	Lemon	Bossier Parish School Board	NAACP	Achievement test scores used for placement of children in newly integrated system

FIGURE 15 (Continued)
COURT CASES INVOLVING STANDARDIZED TESTS

Locale	Plaintiff	Defendant	Organization Assisting Plaintiff	Grievance
Charlotte, N.C.	Singleton	Anson County Board of Education	Justice Department	Desegregation of faculty in-school segregation due to ability grouping
Washington, D.C.	Hobson	Hansen	Peter Rousselot, ACLU	Segregation; unfair distribution of teacher resources between black and white schools
Sacramento, Calif.	Ruiz	California State Board of Education	California Rural Legal Assistance Program	Placement in retarded classes by group IQ tests for any purposes
Salt Lake City, Utah	Wolf	Legislature of the State of Utah	Utah Association for Mentally Retarded Children	Denial of free, public education to mentally retarded children as identified by tests
Milwaukee. Wis.	Doe	Board of School Directors	Freedom Through Equality, Incorporated	Denial of enrollment in trainable mentally retarded class
Boston, Mass.	Stewart	Phillips	Boston Legal Assistance Project	Students denied right to an education by being classified as mentally retarded and placed in "special classes" (students were improperly classified)

or state for two years." This stipulation would allow black in-migrant children from Mississippi to get the feel of Chicago and its culture and schools before any tests are given, with the exception, perhaps, of a locator test for beginning instruction.

A black and brown group of legislators sponsored a bill to prohibit placement of children in special-education programs, unless the results of a complete psychological examination corroborate test score findings that indicate placement in such classes.[3] The bill also requires the written consent of parents to have children placed in special-education classes and limits placement of any pupil to such classes. Of all bills introduced, this piece of legislation is perhaps the best model for black legislators seeking to assure improvements in this area. California lawmakers also sponsored legislation requiring that in cases of bilingual children slated for special-education classes, individual tests be administered in the primary home language of the child.[4] All of these bills are now law in California.

Communities might use the same approaches—petitions and lawsuits—to assure black children and youth equal access to good teachers and curricula in all levels of the school.

Even if a poor child were not placed in a special-education class, he is quite likely to be tracked on the basis of test scores in elementary schools. Tracking, in this sense, means assigning children to classes on the basis of tests. Children are assigned to slow, average, and fast tracks on this basis. Yearly, children in high tracks receive 180 well-planned lessons in the three R's offered by a well-trained, experienced, and well-supervised teacher. The teacher expects substantial performance of the children and makes demands for class performance and homework. Children in low tracks receive less than 180 well-planned lessons, have many more substitute and temporary teachers, and their regular teachers are more often young and inexperienced, older teachers with less refined skills, or teachers with a variety of problems.

In the main, a good school assigns children by alphabetical order. A given classroom resembles the community, with children possessing all sorts of gifts and backgrounds working together. Ideally, the class is nongraded and each child is moving at a pace that suits him; a teacher can expect learning spurts, plateaus, regression, and unusual progress from each pupil. In the good school, too, a spirit of "us" and "we" is fostered. Work groups are important. In these groups, the quick children help the slower children break codes when needed. Children with special gifts and talents and backgrounds make their inputs in the work groups and cooperatively the work gets done. If democracy is to be served, children helping one another should be what the American school is all about. The children prepare to get the work of their communities done by working together in their school groups.

Tracking children militates against this cooperation. The school becomes an arena for child-racing. Parents come to regard the school as a place where their children can get the jump on their neighbor by ingesting a certain percentage of additional information and regurgitating this information—relevant or otherwise—on normative-based tests. Through this apparatus, institutional racism is practiced—the rich get richer and the poor get poorer and get taught their place in life. Middle-class children, black and white, are afforded access to the better teachers, a more enriched and a more thorough curriculum on the basis of entrance tests in the first grade, receive more information, and proceed to make higher test scores throughout school. These advantages assure access to the best the schools have to offer and manifest themselves in even higher terminal school test scores, higher scores in industrial and government job testing, and ultimately better jobs.

Job testing is under heavy fire in the courts. Excellent decisions are being rendered enjoining firms to discontinue the use of tests that reflect access to good teachers and curricula, but that have little or no connection to getting the job done. In a textbook case, some one hundred or so black postal workers were somehow put to work without the usual civil-service test requiring a knowledge of Beowulf's trials and tribulations. After working for a year, all received excellent ratings by their supervisors. The Post Office discovered its error late in the second year and, seeking to set the record straight, required the men to take the test. None passed. A civil-service panel finally ruled that they were entitled to keep their jobs.[5]

Assuring that needed reforms in the schools take place is the challenge to the black community. Again, careful study of the testing-tracking-testing (TTT) syndrome, petitions, and if necessary, lawsuits will serve to bring about this change. Any civic group can take a leadership role. Agenda of legislators of all races can accommodate bills to bring reforms. By 1999, the TTT syndrome should not be a problem in American schools, and a debt of gratitude will be owed civic workers in black communities who brought this change about.

Cradle Schools and Pre-K Programs

Perhaps one of the more fruitful endeavors black civic groups can engage in is a drive to assure slots for 150,000 black children in cradle schools and another 700,000 in pre-K programs. The children involved would come from the poverty-stricken families in black communities. As described in Chapter 2, these programs are highly effective and add the final element to the good school described above: effective ameliorative intervention to enable children to get off to a good start in school.

The price tag for cradle and pre-K programs is high. A billion dollars a year would be necessary for cradle schools for 300,000 children (birth to two years) and $2 billion for preschools (three to five years). A selling job emerges for the black community. Expansion of the Heber and parent-child programs, described earlier, into a national network of living demonstrations would convince many congressmen of the feasibility of making this investment. Just witnessing six-year-olds from poverty families who read and do numbers is enough to convince even the most hardened legislator that a cradle school operation might be worth a month's bombing of some foreign country.

Work will also be needed at the local level to prod local schools or child development agencies to operate these programs properly. Unfortunately, some school leaders regard these programs as dangerous, especially in some communities in the South. Cradle and pre-K programs will serve to remove a valuable weapon racists use to deny blacks access to quality school offerings and to subsequent economic and political competition in community life. These preschool programs develop eager, alert, high-scoring black youngsters who will grow up to be eager, alert, hard-driving adults—the last thing disciples of Theodore Bilbo, the late senator from Mississippi, want in their communities. This realization dawned sickeningly on the writer one sultry afternoon in a Mississippi Delta town after two days as a consultant to a school superintendent who ostensibly wanted to improve the schooling of black children. This man really wanted the federal money for such a program but was intent on developing a program that failed. It did. The only solution in such situations is a thoroughly aware community group that understands clearly what good cradle schools and pre-K programs look like and insists that schools deliver in this area. A national network of demonstration projects will do yeoman's service in this respect.

Black Demography

Important changes are under way in black demography; acceleration of these changes will be beneficial. In the short space of twenty-five years, blacks changed from rural to metropolitan dwellers and made shifts from farming occupations to factory workers and are winnowing large numbers of workers into (or back into) the crafts and into professional and technical ranks. Four million black people moved from the South to the North to bring about a fifty-fifty population concentration in these regions. An amazing transformation, this move tested and is still testing the fiber of the black community.

Black families are also joining the parade toward fewer children per family. The efforts of community groups are reaching into nooks and crannies of depressed areas and bringing the benefits of family planning. Nothing could be more applaudable. In a time when raising and educating a child properly costs

$35,000 ($45,000 with a college degree), black and white parents at all income levels are pausing before they add to their families.

Family size affects academic attainment in myriad ways according to the British study *From Birth to Seven*.[6] The best achieving children come from families of moderate to high income who have one or two children. Figure 16 indicates the

FIGURE 16
FAMILY SIZE AND OTHER FACTORS IN READING ATTAINMENT

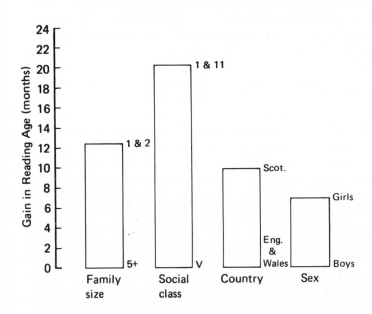

Family size and other factors in reading attainment

SOURCE: Ronald Davie, Neville R. Butler, and Harvey Goldstein, *From Birth to Seven* (London: Longman, 1972), p. 32.

relationship of some of these factors. Family size alone accounts for a twelve-month reading difference when large (five children) and small (one or two children) families are considered. The factors in the graph are also cumulative. Thus, an English boy from social class V and a family of five would fall forty-eight months below a Scottish girl from social class I and a family with one or two children. In this context, the large farm families of bygone years simply will not fit into today's framework of expensive and fast-paced education.

Birth order also has an effect on reading attainment that is nearly as great as social class. Figure 17 demonstrates this concept. If black families mired in poverty were to make choices, the decision to have only one child would be ideal. The difference in reading between first and fourth children is sixteen months and the difference between an only child and the third child of a family of three is twenty-four months.[7] Many factors go into this dynamic—diet, enrichment of life-styles, amount of adult competition, among others. The message to poor parents is clear. Raising and educating a child in today's world is difficult and financially demanding.

Further consideration is warranted to the earlier note on the necessity of black middle- and upper-class families to replace themselves. The family economics of education make this necessity even clearer. Middle- and upper-class black families limit their families to an average of 1.6 children. Replacement rates for families are 2.1. With a 44 percent black middle and upper class, roughly 220,000 children should be born into well-educated families with money to educate these children well and 280,000 children should be born into less fortunate families. With the present 1.6 birthrate for middle- and upper-class black families, however, this projection is not the case. The figures are more like 167,000 children born in these families and 333,000 born to working and poverty-ridden families. A demography that had 300,000 children born to middle- and upper-class families and 200,000 born to others would result in a rapid movement into the middle class.

Although virtually no researchers have controlled for black demography in their studies, these data affect almost every

FIGURE 17
BIRTH ORDER AND OTHER FACTORS IN READING ATTAINMENT

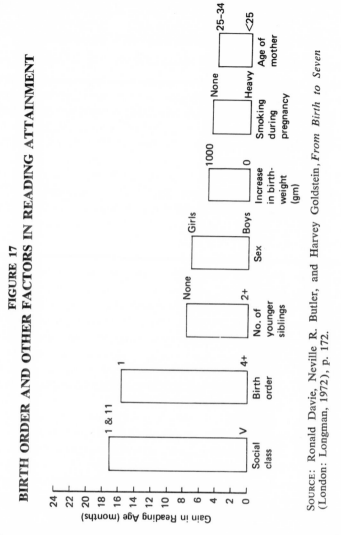

SOURCE: Ronald Davie, Neville R. Butler, and Harvey Goldstein, *From Birth to Seven* (London: Longman, 1972), p. 172.

phase of black-white comparisons. Because of black demographic omission, all studies of achievement, aptitude, and persistence must be reconsidered, and if important enough, the data must be reanalyzed.

Black family job demography might also be altered in this drive and seems a worthy goal. In addition to having approximately twice as many children per family as middle- and upper-class blacks, poverty-ridden families—black and white—have lessened wage earning power because of demography. Middle- and upper-class blacks provide 155 workers for every 100 families in this group. These workers include 90 males, 10 single, separated, widowed, or divorced females, and 55 work- ing wives. Blacks and whites in the poverty categories only muster 135 workers per hundred families. These 135 workers include 70 males, 30 single, separated, widowed, or divorced females, and 35 working wives. The 20 point difference in total workers plus the 20 point difference in male workers affects income considerably. Men workers earn 40 percent more than women workers.

Bigotry, an inordinate share (52 percent) of Southern families where income lags generally for blacks and whites, plus black family job demography combine to create gaps between black family income and national averages. For example, 535,000 young black married families with two workers exceed their white counterparts in earning power and exceed the national average by 8 percent.[8]

In fairness, a huge share of the blame for imbalance in male wage earners in poverty groups must be laid at the feet of Northern planners of welfare programs. Southern poverty fami- lies have a much larger percentage of male workers. Many observers have opined that much of the early Northern welfare laws and guidelines may have been developed by antimale women—female chauvinists. Northern welfare laws for years drove male wage earners from the household.[9] Some states still have such laws requiring the absence of husbands, lovers, teen- age working sons, male relatives, boarders, or any other men who might go out and bring in a few dollars for which welfare may have been either a supplement or a base to be supple- mented. The men must go and the family is awarded a pittance representing about 25 percent of the national average income. The signal for both the black and the white community is to reduce welfare needs by pushing for jobs for men and women, equal pay for women, and a revised welfare law developed by sane, intelligent people.

Schools That Serve and Not Rule the People

Paul Dimond ends an article in a monograph of the Harvard University Center for Law and Education by noting that "each child or parent who walks into a law office complaining about a school classification requires redress for himself and represents the first opportunity to look deeper into a school system with many more students like him. The objective is simple: make the schools, administrators, counselors and teachers serve the family, not rule it. Many school classification practices do exactly the opposite." [10]

Dimond points out that until the American schools' system of testing, sorting, tracking, and other forms of class and caste perpetuation is effectively challenged, the myths and widely held belief of democratic, public common schools will effectively camouflage this sad situation and in effect perpetuate the failures of our schools to serve children well. Dimond states that the key to any ultimate reform in this situation is the awakening of consumers of educational services to real facts about how schools work. He notes that the process of awakening may be made to happen through litigation that is publicly instructive and by pressing for legislative and administrative reform.

Dimond might have added that community involvement and control of schools are effective devices for enabling poor blacks to make certain their schools serve and not rule them. He might have added that the schools should stop sorting and labeling poor black children, teaching them what and when they please, shunting them into programs leading to economic genocide, and resisting any parental influence on the process. Educators with a central office rule book stipulating all school practices to be required or prohibited and requiring anything new to have been done before must be eliminated.

More black parents in depressed areas are demanding that schools be of the community as well as in it. The days when a faculty or thirty or so teachers can commute to a building and effectively decide on the destiny of a thousand future adults by the application of school practices that are injurious to their aspirations and development are about passed.

Community control of schools has always been a fact in affluent communities. Teachers and administrators serve these communities as public servants to render a service and are respected, even revered, in the community for doing this job well. Schoolteachers and administrators somehow bridle at the idea of serving poor communities in a similar manner. A psychological problem exists here, seemingly bound up in social pecking orders and matters of self-esteem. The first step in developing effective schools in these poor areas, perhaps, would be selection of personnel with as few psychological biases as possible and the offering of awareness sessions for those finally selected for service in the schools.

An effective school board uses community advisory groups for all programs including the selection of a superintendent. The process of decision making is slowed somewhat but schools serve people better as a result. In a single year, the board may have received and acted on three nominations for principals emanating from a search committee comprised of a central office representative and two members of the community advisory board of each school. The board may also have acted on principal and advisory board recommendations for a new system of testing, a new high-impact program, and denial of permission to a local college or university to conduct research of doubtful design and value. In reaching the latter decision, the principal and advisory committee may have availed themselves of experts concerned about research abuse in the black community.

Many school systems, such as one in Philadelphia, have utilized community control as a mechanism for developing small school districts and thus making schools more responsive to communities. Even though smaller districts were created and finally developed, New York experienced resistance from the central office and, oddly, from a teachers union.

High on the agenda for black communities might well be a concerted effort to bring about control over what is going on in schools where their children are enrolled. Oddly, the higher the percentage of black children and the higher the percentage of white faculty, the more important parental involvement becomes.

The experience of black middle-class parents at the Windsor Hills School in Los Angeles is a case in point. Windsor Hills enrolled children from high-aspiring, upwardly mobile, and hard-driving black families. The school's children had the highest average IQ in the city (116) in 1969. The struggle these parents had with the superintendent of Los Angeles and his staff to maintain quality education at Windsor Hills destroys any faith in the beautiful rhetoric school administrators and professors can spin about community and school partnerships as the backbone of American democracy. Windsor Hills School was built in 1954 and served a totally white community ranging from middle class to millionaires. The facility was operated as a school and community center, serving as a meeting place for Boy Scouts, Girl Scouts, and Camp Fire Girls. A ballroom dance class was offered for sixth graders. The class was offered by a private dance studio but arranged through the school. Over the years, the only ruffle in the serenity of Windsor Hills was the quiet fight to turn back the bid of a Jewish candidate for P.T.A. president. This defeat was done in typical Windsor Hills fashion, by proxy votes in a half-empty meeting hall.[11]

Then, the black families came to Windsor Hills. Their children were denied memberships in the Boy Scouts, Girl Scouts, Camp Fire Girls, and the dancing school. Whites began moving out. By 1961 black enrollment reached 30 percent at Windsor Hills, and by 1963 the school was mostly black. For a while the school situation moved along well. Homes in Windsor Hills cost $50,000, and in Baldwin Hills (a feeder community where whites fled and blacks followed) homes were in the $70,000 to $100,000 range. School achievement remained high and Windsor Hills School went along its placid way.

One day, however, the assistant superintendent for elementary schools told the Windsor Hills principal that Windsor Hills would be placed on double shifts because of the overcrowding of Los Angeles schools. A parents' group was formed and spent a year and a half fighting this threat. This group even attempted to defray the cost of setting up mobile classrooms but were told that this was not allowable. Sheer pressure plus a weeding out of students who should not have been at Windsor Hills because of the location of their residences finally staved off double shifts.

Then came a hassle about the gifted children's program for the area. Although Windsor Hills provided twenty-two out of the twenty-six gifted children in the program, the central office based the program at a neighboring school. The Windsor Hills' parents demanded that the program operate at Windsor Hills. They demanded that children on the waiting list be tested and the program expanded. The final outcome was abandonment of the entire program by the central office.

The central office then proceeded to dismantle the music program and the library. The latter was finally restored after much protest. In a situation that arose where an extra teacher was allocated to Windsor Hills, the central office assigned a physical education teacher and the children are getting extra work in physical fitness, not music or art or science. The lesson is that even in a good neighborhood, a racist school administration will make a determined effort to systematically undermine excellence if the school is black. If black parents from professional and business backgrounds had to fight this hard to maintain standards at Windsor Hills, think of what working-class blacks must be up against.

Regardless, precisely these groups, black working-class parents and those without jobs, must form the muscle to assure schools that serve the people. Programs that promote awareness of the elements of good and bad schools will enable these groups to effectively contend for their children's education.

Simple but essential elements of a good school that are easily understood by anyone might comprise the core of a program designed to promote awareness. The following might find a place on such a list:

1. Class sizes of twenty to twenty-two in the primary grades and twenty-five in upper grades
2. Thirty percent of the teachers with master's degrees
3. Substitute-teacher days at or below district average

4. Teacher turnover at or below district average
5. A program for gifted children
6. Effective teaching of phonics
7. Evaluation of each teacher on a value-added basis; that is, given twenty-two to twenty-five children in September, what growth has been achieved as a result of her tutelage—what value has been added
8. IQ tests not in use; instead, locator and criterion tests used extensively
9. Blacks in leadership positions, though not exclusively so
10. A curriculum with a black perspective

A black working-class community group can disseminate this information widely. The objectives are readily understood and appreciated. The group can use the list as a context in which to consider the affairs of their school. The items can serve as a list of minimum essentials (LME) around which to rally. In the course of meetings, readings, discussions, and use of consultants, other aspects can be added. The LME is a good basic starting point for a group, however.

The federal government made a good start in promoting community involvement by requiring a parent advisory committee for many of its programs to assist needy children. This program might well be expanded. Many school districts use the new federal money coming into their communities to rule the people more effectively. Sorting programs are strengthened by purchases of even more biased tests. Districts that could not afford the planned and systematic educational retardation of special-education classes can now add these programs. New vocational classes that train for jobs that do not exist must have an average daily membership. Good, solid, phonics-based reading instruction can now be replaced by a program developed for children in a school system far away. But with added federal dollars, a record of innovation must be established.

One of the first items on the agenda of the black parent group might be a review of Titles I and III of the Elementary and Secondary Education Act to ascertain if these programs contribute to the achievement of the LME or whether they actually work against these goals. Although this may seem astounding, as described above, school administrators could actually use federal programs against the goals of achievement. Further in this review might be a consideration of the actual misuse of federal funds in schools. As mentioned earlier, the Washington Research Project has documented many cases of this fraud. Only an alert community group can serve as a restraining influence on what seems to be inordinate duplicity on the part of an alarming number of school administrators and a warped set of priorities on the part of others.[12]

Still other educators, and perhaps a majority, have no idea at all of how to vary a school program to meet the needs of disadvantaged or minority children. As college entrance records show, school administrators and teachers, by and large, but with many notable exceptions, are not the most able and imaginative professionals. Taught a way of doing things in their training programs, many are unable to deviate from this way, although they may want to do so. This failure to adapt accounts in a large measure for the popularity of performance contracting and voucher systems. People believe more able personnel work at IBM or Westinghouse than in educational systems. Educators ought to take righteous umbrage at this stereotyping and set about the creativity that will change their image.

With all hands pushing to reshape the role of the schools in many communities, expanded efforts in the black community might bear fruit more quickly than is realized. Ivan Illich, author of *Deschooling Society,* is pressing for an abolition of schools entirely.[13] A general reconsideration of the place of schools in the scheme of things is needed. Schools that serve—not rule—might be possible to bring about in any community. In intractable situations such as the abandoning of the gifted children's program in Windsor Hills, blacks might combine with whites, who have branded schools a monopoly operated with public funds, and push for a voucher system of public education.

Presently financed on an experimental basis in a handful of communities by the Office of Economic Opportunity, vouchers provide for parents to be awarded payment of the average pupil costs of their district and purchase schooling for the children at a public or private school of their choice. In the case of the Windsor Hills and Baldwin Hills parents, they would have been given a voucher for $1,000 each to set up classes for gifted children or enroll their children in a school, public or private, that offered this work. A fine variation on this theme would be the award of $500 each to the parents to hire science, math, and fine arts teachers for half-day sessions in a wing of the building or a portable annex. The students would attend regular classes for physical education, social studies, and reading. Vouchers can be quite disturbing and they are not new. Virginia used a voucher system as a safety valve for bigots who were determined to fight integrated schools. Segregated academies sprang up, and for a while the state spent several million dollars each year operating private, segregated schools with public money. Even demands and new laws requiring integration of the schools produced little in this respect. What black student wants to attend a school named after George Wallace or other racists, flying a Rebel flag, and playing "Dixie" on the Muzak?

On the other hand, large numbers of whites used vouchers to enroll their children in integrated private schools, in integrated schools in neighboring districts, or to send them out of state. Some white parents used vouchers to send their children to Hampton Institute's campus school, rated one of the ten best schools in the country by experts on nongraded schools. Black parents also used a large number of vouchers. They sent their children to better black schools and to well-integrated schools in neighboring districts or out of state. The real solution in American education is for educators to develop schools that truly serve the people.

Research on White Racism

Civilization sank to all-time lows during Nazi atrocities at the gas ovens and the atrocities of Alabama, Mississippi, and other Deep South states during the lynching era. The lynch mob, whether at Auschwitz or Sunflower County, Mississippi, represented man gone mad. W. J. Cash, a white Southern writer with keen perception and an acute anguish over the condition of his people, wrote one of the early books on what makes the racist run. His volume, *The Mind of the South,* delved deeply into the Southern psyche, sorting out grinding poverty, boll weevils, floods, pellagra, towering ignorance, and fears of black male sexual prowess as factors combining to drive a Southern dirt farmer or filling-station worker to load his wife and children into a mule-drawn wagon and drive into town to attend a lynching bee.[14] Cash documented the powerful impact of racism on whites with analyses of the contents of nightmares and hallucinations of the emotionally disturbed and the mutterings of the old and senile. Race dominated these deranged minds to an overwhelming extent.

Cash even toyed with the idea of some dysgenic trend as a cause of racism. According to this theory, blood lust might be found to become acute according to some lunar cycle. He also noted that 90 per cent of pre-Reconstruction lynchees were white.

Cash died prematurely at the age of thirty-six. *Mind of the South* was a book that was but a prelude, it seemed, to the genius this young man was capable of unfolding. One can only surmise what direction both the South and his life and career might have taken. The only certainty is both would have been interesting—and dangerous. Many Southerners wanted to lynch Cash.

Mind of the South made a heavy impact on both the intellectual and business communities of the South and was a force in expanding the cadres of moderates in this region that finally brought an end to lynching and drove the South to accept civil-rights laws with some modicum of grace. For example, the 1972 Louisiana legislature, in a symbolic gesture, repealed all of its old Jim Crow laws.

Another W. J. Cash is needed in these times to study and explicate the racist mind. The old-time lynching bee is no longer a part of Southern life, but the effects of racism on both blacks and whites is just as devastating. Racism hampers every aspect of the life and aspirations of the former and has a degrading and degenerating effect on these elements for the latter.

The axiom of prejudice being directed most intensely at groups on the rise is apropos. While blacks are making fine strides ahead and while the general trend in the country is toward racial moderation, racism can be said to be intensifying in some quarters. This phenomenon needs study and explication, and possible cures to the situation need wide dissemination.

Black researchers are going to have to carry out much of this research. A W. J. Cash comes along only once in a generation or so. Most whites do not have this sort of perception or sensitivity. Many researchers are racists themselves. Constraints and pressures of social groups preclude serious research and reporting on racism by whites. Most settle matters of conscience by joining groups overstudying the victim.

Men like Price Cobbs, James Comer, and Edward Barnes, able black clinicians, might well be pressed into service by the National Institutes of Health to lead research on this illness. The NIH and other foundations have a responsibility to make ample funds available and to seek these men. Many program and project officers at NIH and the foundations are racist and will be reluctant to fund research by blacks in this area. Some are given pause by blacks studying whites. The black agenda might deal with this situation. Government research funds to study racism—the nation's most serious mental illness—seems a worthy expenditure at this juncture in the nation's history.

Research designs in racism will be interesting and, if done well, will yield insightful and useful findings. The studies will also have to be intricate. Racists do not hitch up the mules and set out for the lynching bee in today's scenario. They crouch behind code words and duplicity, using clever stratagems to violate laws relating to jobs, housing, and schools. The same fear and bitterness that drove wild-eyed Southern mobs generate much of the racism today. Fear of rule by another tribe, the black sex thing, job insecurity, loss of equity in housing investments, and fear of black violence are all factors that will have to be sorted and for which ameliorative strategies will have to be devised and tested.

Charles McCabe, for example, the respected *San Francisco*

Chronicle columnist, relates Northern racism of immigrant groups to the shift of emphasis from melting pot to ethnicity. McCabe terms this change of emphasis as a way of saying to blacks and browns that "there is no longer any room at the Inn." [15] McCabe recalled the emphasis on the melting pot in his youth and how in spite of Irish, Italians, and Jews fighting each other, the general consensus was to "get everybody in." Now McCabe contends that people do not talk about the melting pot much anymore. He may have added that two gentlemen who made it via the pot (Nathan Glazer and Daniel Moynihan) wrote a recent and influential book, *Beyond the Melting Pot,* claiming, among other things, that the melting pot never really existed at all. McCabe claims that too often today, among the Germans and Swedes who made it into the pot around the turn of the century and the other groups who were able to clamber in later, the stress on ethnicity is not to get everybody in but to keep everybody out. He deplores this syndrome. He notes with irony that some quite vigorous efforts to do this kind of exclusion come from some ethnic groups who themselves are not entirely in the pot.

In trying to analyze why this discrimination has happened, McCabe makes some of the same theories for his immigrant groups that W. J. Cash made for his pellagra-ridden dirt farmers of English stock. The difference is that guilt is added to the equation and economic and sexual fears are pushed up front. "The recent immigrant strain is the most intolerant," McCabe contends, "because we have the most to lose. A colored man is bad enough. A colored man who is strong enough and smart enough to take our job away from us and maybe our wife too, is quite literally beyond the pale. This is what a fearsome society has done to the great idea of the melting pot." McCabe goes on to show the role guilt plays in racism. "You can never like something you're guilty about. We are guilty, and terribly, about the way we act about color because we know our country was not meant to be this way." [16] McCabe and Cash expound theories that may explain unions that practice economic genocide on black craftsmen, real estate operators who attend classes on stratagems to evade fair-housing laws, and leeches who hate minorities but are determined to get a cut of the funds appropriated by the government to the disadvantaged.

Some of the smartest men in the country ought to be set to the task of lessening these fears and guilt through research and explication. For blacks and other colored minorities, of course, the demise of the melting pot leaves them in a position of having to rally around their own racial identities and cultures and gnaw into the pot from without. Many whites are inside the pot gnawing out and trying to help minorities. One saving grace remains. Colored minorities will be able to enter the mainstream without sacrificing their cultures. Said differently, blacks will not have to "Anglocize" themselves as many of the melting pot people did.

Elements of pride and self-respect can be touched in research on racism, just as Cash touched pride and self-respect in *Mind of the South*. The Teamsters, a large union, recently protested vigorously that Archie Bunker was an exercise in the stereotyping of working whites. The union noted—and rightly so— that all working-class whites were not bigots and that the Bunker television portrayal caused pain and suffering to working-class whites committed to human rights and racial equality. Effective research on white racism and wide media dissemination would reveal to many whites feelings long suppressed and sublimated. Moreover, such research would promote an awareness that would serve to lessen many racist practices and enable civil-rights' laws to work more effectively with offenders.

In schools and colleges, such research could be extremely helpful. Probably more racists exist in higher education than one imagines. Someone once said that higher education is like grade A milk—rich, white, and homogenized. Though no longer the case, higher education is now the most segregated education in existence. Black youth seeking to expand black participation in the enterprise have found tough sledding on many campuses. Racism on campuses seems inversely proportionate to the social class of white students, college faculty, employees, and the social class of the college. Black students at Yale, therefore, have little difficulty with racism. At the University of Connecticut they have considerable problems. At Michigan State, little trouble exists; but at Ferris State, also in Michigan, there is fighting in the streets.

A good start on promoting awareness of racist school practices has been made by centers concerned with problems related to desegregation of Southern schools. These centers were funded under Title IV of the Civil-Rights Act of 1964. Some of the centers have been highly effective and their work can be emulated in every school system enrolling black students. An example of an effective center is the Consultative Resources Center of the University of Virginia. This center was headed for six years by James Bash, and its work was important in the peaceful desegregation of Virginia schools. Peaceful desegregation was especially important in rural south-central Virginia where pockets of bigotry still feed on the memories of white losses during the Nat Turner slave rebellion of 1831. Bash, a native of Kokomo, Indiana, was principal of Prince Edward County High School in Virginia. He was fired from his job after suggesting that schools in the county integrate peacefully. Prince Edward finally closed all of its schools for a period of four years, and only under the astute maneuvering of a new governor, Albertis Harrison, was the county forced to reinstate public education.

In six years of operation, the University of Virginia center held workshops on school desegregation in every school district and involved every superintendent in intensive planning designed to make the transition to unitary schools effective. Almost every effective existing piece of material on race relations and prejudice was utilized in the process. Entire faculties were touched and some city and county governments enrolled their employees. Bash and his twelve associates—mostly former superintendents and principals—also did effective research on human relations dynamics and much of this research is continuing today.

The important contribution of desegregation centers is perhaps the enunciation of simple dos and don'ts of race relations and the development of materials that are circulated widely. The writer and Armin Beck of the University of Illinois, Chicago Circle Campus, were retained as consultants several years ago to develop a racial eitquette guide for a community in the South-east that planned to integrate its schools. The city fathers were concerned about fighting in the high schools and the prospects of ripple effects in the community. City officials had decided to work through the Urban Coalition to reach a large number of community groups. The authors of the guide decided to stress fifteen simple mistakes that cause things to go awry in integrated schools and to stress student pride in carrying off a peaceful plan of integration. Practical though it was, the guide got at many of Cash's generators of racial hate: a lost war, clannishness, stereotypy. The Brazziel-Beck Etiquette Guide is included below.

Etiquette for Integrated Schools

Some of our recently integrated schools are models of racial harmony and racial respect. Others are marred by tension and, sometimes, violence.

Why is this? What can be done to assure a smooth integration process? Authorities who have studied these situations often point out unconscious faux pas and mistakes in conversations and actions by students and teachers as the chief source of discord. It behooves us, then, to become aware of the most common errors and to guard against them. Thus this guide to etiquette for our unitary schools.

1. Authorities now believe that racial harmony is achieved most easily when stress on race in conversations and interaction is minimal. Try to think of Mary Jones as a junior student instead of Mary Jones, a white junior student, or Mary Jones, a black junior student. Try speaking in this manner in the cafeteria and on the bus. Write this way in your newspaper. It will soon become a part of you.

2. Schools can operate very effectively over long periods of time without reference to racial designations, but sometimes these are necessary. When this is the case, the terms *white* and *Caucasian* and *black* or *Negro* are

proper. If *Negro* is used, practice to make sure it does not come out "Nigra." This is an insult to most black people. Practice: *Knee-Grow.* Use of the term *cracker* is to be avoided although some Southern white people wear the name proudly.

3. Avoid referring to others in a racial group as *you, you people,* or *you all.*

4. Avoid patronizing sayings such as "some of my best friends are . . ." (white, colored, Jewish, Polish, etc.).

5. Do not tell ethnic jokes.

6. If "Dixie" is to be played by the school band, suggest to your band director that he follow a growing practice in unitary schools by following up with "We Shall Overcome." Good will is the key here.

7. The United States flag—alone—should fly over your building. If the Confederate flag also flies, open a discussion of this in the student council.

8. Expect basic Southern courtesy from everyone you meet in the school. If you expect it, you will get it most of the time.

9. Some ill-bred people will be discourteous. Look at this on a percentage basis and suggest that they move to New York or Mississippi.

10. Call all of the cafeteria and custodial staff by courtesy titles regardless of race.

11. Make sure that whichever race is a minority in the school is also well represented in student activities and athletics. If none are in your activities, invite some of your acquaintances to join. Sponsor them if necessary.

12. Work hard together across racial lines on long projects. Authorities have found this a sure-fire means of reducing racial tension. The projects can be almost anything— in class or out.

13. Make sure leaders from whichever is a minority group in the school have the opportunity to assume a share of the leadership positions.

14. Argue with persons of another race. It is refreshing and

relaxes tension. Do not fight, however, unless it is absolutely unavoidable.

15. Be proud of the racial harmony and cooperation in your school. If it is something to boast about, do so. It is a state of being that all of America is striving for today.

Again, research and explication of psychological generators of racism seem applicable at this juncture. Black researchers must be responsible for the initiatives because of social and sometimes psychological strictures of white researchers. Many able black clinicians are in this field. Impetus must be given through the grants of the National Institute of Mental Health and the foundations and the U.S. Office of Education.

Community Programs for Gifted Children and Youth

A close-knit black community near Great Bridge, Virginia, sends a large number of well-prepared young people to college. The performance of these youngsters in college is excellent, although most all are first generation college students. Their persistence in school outstrips national averages and a sophisticated system of financial support undergirds their efforts.

This community revolves around a church of one of the lesser-known denominations. The church operates a farm and marketing cooperative, and other income comes from their workers and craftsmen operating throughout the Hampton Roads area.

Brilliant children are identified early in this community, and the people understand that these children will go to college regardless of their family finances. The church provides a stipend and provides every type of information and assistance on federal, state, and private sources of support.

Every opportunity is given these children to develop their talents in this community. The children are given intellectual responsibilities designed to bring out and strengthen every potential. Talented youngsters teach younger children in Sunday school and summer Bible classes. At twelve years of age or so, they are periodically invited to teach the adult classes. Extensive pageants are expected of these children at Thanksgiving, Christmas, Easter, and Children's Day. On the farms, they are expected to compute the weights and measures. A steady rain of cultural tours emanate from their planning. Williamsburg, Yorktown Battlefield, Jamestown, Shenandoah, and Washington, D.C., find an annual place on the docket. Summer visits and study with relatives and former church members all over the country broaden their horizons.

Community expectations for success of these gifted children are high. The children are taught to regard their talents as a gift that must be developed fully and then shared with their community. A large number of college graduates either return to their community to serve it or keep close contacts and help with new generations of gifted children.

This concern for talent development is remarkable but such a concern has long been a hallmark of black community groups. Such concern must be cultivated and expanded, especially in depressed areas in Northern cities, which received four million displaced rural blacks over the past two decades.

The black churches, lodges, and civic and social groups have a great responsibility. At every annual convention, the topic of community programs for gifted children might find a place on the agenda. The challenging experiences afforded by an entire community of people are invaluable, as is the assurance of financial support and the motivation of high community expectations. This involvement is a game any group can play. The involvement ranges from the more spectacular operations like Wilberforce University; the African Methodist Episcopal School, which boasts of students from thirty-eight states and ten foreign countries (most sent by churches); to the efforts of Delta Sigma Theta, a black sorority in an Eastern city, which awards two $2,000 scholarships annually; and the Midwestern local of the Amalgamated Meat Packers and Butcher Workers of North America, which awards one.

Gifted disadvantaged children need to be afforded a wide variety of contacts with middle-class professionals and artists in their communities. This contact is stimulating, widens the perceptions of the children about options available to them, and enables them to understand routes to professional and artistic goals. The contact also generates a vast, informal network of informal assistance involving the professionals and artists. Opportunities for summer enrichment programs, jobs, camps, scholarships, admission to alma maters, trips, and participation in community activities bubble up from these contacts.

The story of two gifted young mathematicians from a depressed area in Norfolk, Virginia, aptly illustrates the dynamics and rewards of expanded contact with middle-class professionals. The incident also demonstrates the roles a community-oriented college, a civic group, and many black and white professionals played in assuring success for these youngsters where every indicator predicted that their talents would have never been developed. These youngsters were born and raised in the most depressed community in Norfolk. They wound up at eighteen years of age in Harvard Yard with advanced placement in Harvard's sophomore math and physics courses and a place on the dean's list. Many institutions and people helped them get to Harvard.

The youngsters' talents were spotted early by elementary schoolteachers at Henry Clay School. Tales of their aptitude were relayed to both the Norfolk Committee on the Improvement of Education (NCIE) and to professors and staff at Norfolk State College, a four-year college with a strong community involvement. Students from Norfolk State involved in freshman year observation and participation in the schools carried the word.

NCIE is an integrated civic group comprised primarily of professional people with a fine mix of community-spirited workers. The thrust of the organization is basically to put pressure on the school board to improve schooling opportunities for black children and to put pressure on the black community to strive even harder for excellence. At the time, NCIE was led by Vivian Carter Mason, an able black woman. Cochairpersons from NCIE both hailed from the local college, and regular meetings of NCIE were held at the college plus a bewildering array of conferences, workshops, committee meetings, and enrichment activities.

The black mathematical geniuses were quickly tucked under the protective wing of the gifted-child committee of NCIE. The resources of the college and access to the most gifted artists and professionals in the city immediately opened up to them. The children were involved in planning enrichment programs for other city children. They heard the speeches of nationally recognized blacks urging them to study hard and develop their talents. They were allowed to observe and help out in the college computer center. The testing bureau introduced them to the mysteries of measurement and statistics. They played math theory games with the professors.

When the youngsters reached junior high school, Mary Johnson, an able mathematician and teacher, was waiting to begin their preparation for college and careers in earnest. Under Mrs. Johnson's tutelage, the youngsters blossomed. Work at the college computer center became more serious. Dr. Marion Capps, director of the testing bureau at Norfolk State, set the young men to working up statistical profiles. Clyde McDaniel of the math department invited them to participate as guests in summer NDEA workshops in math. The boys spent many hours at the Johnson and Mason homes as dinner guests and sometimes as contractors for construction and repair work.

At Booker T. Washington High School, James Johnson, a physicist and the second member of the Johnson team, and Serelda James, dean of the city schools' mathematicians, took over. Mrs. James took the boys to New Mexico for a summer institute she taught in mathematics. Mr. Johnson opened up contacts with the college's physics department and began to prepare the boys for their College Boards. The young geniuses made nearly perfect scores on quantitative aptitude and on achievement tests in mathematics and physics.

At this point, Adam Clymer, a Harvard alumni and staunch member of NCIE, interceded. He contacted one of the deans of Harvard College and everything was downhill all the way from that point.

This success story began with students from a metropolitan

college with a strong community involvement and with teachers and civic groups utilizing the resources of the institution. The college was never central in any of this saga, but an easy guess is that some 50 percent of the contacts, exposure, encouragement, and assistance came from people employed at the college or happened in the facilities of the college. What would happen if our twelve hundred community colleges rolled up their sleeves and warmed to the task of generating the identification, involvement, contacts, enrichment, warmth, and assistance needed by gifted minority children with the terrifying odds of a bad environment arrayed against them?

Efforts at talent development in many black communities are remarkable. These efforts must be expanded. Gifted children in every community must be afforded the benefits of challenging experiences, community guidance and support, plus the motivational impetus of high community expectations. Black churches and civic groups and black individuals have a responsibility here, and every respect and accolade must be given to those who perform well in this respect.

Notes for Chapter 7

[1] "Court Suits Involving Standardized Tests." Mimeographed. National Leadership Institute in Teacher Education, University of Connecticut, 1972.

[2] California Legislature, Senate Bill No. 987, April 23, 1972.

[3] California Legislature, Senate Bill No. 33, January 5, 1971.

[4] California Legislature, Senate Bill No. 1317, April 8, 1970.

[5] Reginald Jones, ed., *Black Psychology* (New York: Harper and Row, 1972), p. 20.

[6] Ronald Davie and Neville R. Butler, *From Birth to Seven* (London: Longman, 1972), p. 32.

[7] *Ibid.*, p. 172.

[8] Ben J. Wattenberg and Richard M. Scammon, "Black Progress and Liberal Rhetoric," *Commentary* (April, 1973), pp. 35–44.

[9] Andrew Billingsley, *Black Families in White America* (Englewood Cliffs, N.J.: Prentice-Hall, Inc., 1968), p. 14.

[10] Paul Dimond, "Classification Practices: A Lawyer's Guide to Schools," *Classification Materials* (Cambridge, Massachusetts:

Harvard Center for Law and Education, 1972).

[11] Olive Walker, "The Windsor Hills School Story," *Integrated Education* (May–June, 1970), pp. 1–3.

[12] *Title I: Is It Serving to Educate Poor Children?* Washington Research Project, 1970.

[13] Ivan Illich, *Deschooling Society* (New York: Harper-Row, 1972).

[14] W. J. Cash, *The Mind of the South* (New York: Alfred A. Knopf, 1941).

[15] *San Francisco Chronicle,* August 9, 1972, p. 9.

[16] *San Francisco Chronicle,* op. cit.

CHAPTER 8

Effective Evaluation of Progress

A SUPERINTENDENT of a medium-size Midwestern school system was disconsolate. Every possible move had been made to improve the schooling of the children in his district. He had reasonable class sizes, good dedicated teachers, and good race relations. Plenty of work existed in his city for all and the pay was high. Nevertheless, his district was ranked at the forty-eighth percentile, down from a previous high of the fifty-eighth percentile on national test score norms. Board members were disgruntled and news writers with limited knowledge of psychometrics were becoming critical in the local press. The superintendent was about convinced that he would have to sell the house, bundle up the children, and start again elsewhere, taking a record of failure with him.

At a lunch with three influential board members, the superintendent, and key staff, the author suggested an analysis of the changing demography of the town and a historical analysis of test scores according to working groups. In a single afternoon, the staff dug up data showing what many school administrators are beginning to recognize. Suburban developments were siphoning off families with few children and educated breadwinners. Craftsmen and workers, most with large families, were becoming the overwhelming majority in the city and their children the overwhelming majority in the schools.

The staff identified another piece of startling data. The working-class children were not only scoring at their historical average on tests, but they had exceeded this average during the past two years.

The researchers next took a look at graduation rates: they

were up. Dropout rates were down, and study after high school was up. The working-class children were getting a better education in the system than they ever had before. In fact, the departure of white-collar children for the suburbs had been a boon. Working-class children now comprised the majority of classes for the gifted and college-bound tracks. They made up the academic clubs, honor societies, and class-officer ranks. In previous years, white-collar students would have shouldered working-class children from this access to the best the schools could offer. Athletics would have been the main area into which most blue-collar children would have been shunted.

The superintendent was finally able to set minds straight about his system by using effective and accurate evaluations of progress. Other school systems and the federal government might do the same. Ineffective and inaccurate evaluation of school programs and school progress is probably the knottiest problem in education. Ineffective and inaccurate evaluation is bound up in a myriad web of factors, not the least of which is plain ignorance of what schools are and what they should do.

First is the disciple factor. Disciples of various strategies and philosophies muddy the water. Other disciples set a goal of Princeton for every child and become angered when all school districts fail to reach this goal. Schooling is declared a failure and public agitation emerges for reform in the direction of goals of the disciples.

Headstart suffered from this syndrome. More than thirteen million volunteer workers were marshaled in the first year of this program. The First Lady of the United States led the drive. Half a million children were enrolled in classes in a span of four months or so. This enrollment represented one of the greatest mobilizations of social energy since World War II and one of the biggest and most effective programs of child development education ever. Children in the program gained ten points on IQ tests in the full-year programs and a big jump on previous performances in learning to read. The nation, feeling good about Headstart, was driving hard to enroll every poor child in a preschool program and to change its elementary school curriculum and teaching with the companion Follow Through program.

Then disciples of "family strategies" entered the picture. In the fourth year of Headstart, a White House advisor seized on one of the many evaluations of Headstart programs and began the process of "destruction by media." First, public circulation of the evaluation was prohibited. Second, the impression was given that the report contained damaging data that had to be reverified. Third, dribbles of the "damaging data" were leaked to now-panting reporters. Fourth, headlines shouted "Headstart Ineffective."

Truth squads finally corrected the misimpressions sowed by these techniques by pointing out the good parts of the study, the general flaws in design, and the fact that Headstart administrators already knew the "damaging data" (summer Headstart programs are far less effective than full-year programs). Nevertheless, public enthusiasm had been dampened and gloom deepened. Three assassinations, riots, war, and a stalled antipoverty war caused many to lose heart and give up on the country.

Then there is the case of a writer of glib articles and books on American schools who wrote an article for one of the most influential liberal magazines in the country (*The New Republic*) charging that no progress had been made in the drive to improve the schooling of minorities, claiming that all ideas and schemes had been exhausted, and generally washing his hands of the matter. In the same month, the U.S. Office of Education was sponsoring a national fair heralding progress in the education of minorities and placing fascinating projects and programs on display. The U.S. Census Bureau was releasing reports about the "impressive gains" in education blacks were making, and the U.S. Labor Department was reporting impressive gains in jobs and housing.

One cannot leave this topic, of course, without mentioning once again the student-run journal that opened its pages to a California racist to attack compensatory education and brand the program a failure. The academic community gnawed on this bone for two years, much to the dismay of both the public and their teachers and administrators, many of whom had developed impressive programs.

What, then, is a good evaluation of success in the drive to

offer quality education for black Americans? How can we avoid judging success for failure? How can we avail ourselves of needed feedback and the motivation that such feedback brings?

Effective evaluation is always developed in the context of goals and objectives of programs. A drive for quality education for black Americans, like all drives, must have special evaluations designed to assess its progress. Situational contexts are unique. Evaluation also can be conceptualized as process evaluation and product evaluation. The former assesses inputs made to achieve goals and the latter deals with products or outputs of the program. Both process and product evaluation are important. A school district might assure a black community group that all hands are making every effort to improve reading and arithmetic and that results will be available in several years.

In the interest of the community, however, one must study closely the inputs made to reach these goals. Installation of programs that are experimental or that have failed widely, for example, constitutes a bad input. Process evaluation can be used to bring about the installation of programs that have a record of success. A combination of clear goals and time frames, excellent process and product evaluation, plus good feedback to the public will constitute effective evaluation of progress in the drive toward quality education.

Clear Goals and Time Frames

Possible goals and time frames have been discussed in previous chapters. These goals should be pulled together and a time frame for their achievement set. The goal and time frame should be slated as the following:

1. A goal of 80 percent high-school graduation by 1980
2. A 100 percent high-school graduation rate by 1999
3. A college graduation rate of 20 percent of the twenty-four-to-twenty-nine-year-old group by 1999
4. Quality continuing education for 70 percent of adults over twenty-five by 1999

5. Twenty thousand black physicians and thirty thousand black lawyers in the work force by 1999

These five goals are specific and their time frames clear. They are quantified and easily measured. They are comprehensive and they are enmeshed in economic contexts. If reached, they would result in trained manpower to fuel the drive toward black-white economic comparability. Most important, perhaps, the goals lend themselves to annual audits, thereby nullifying charges of no progress by naysayers and proponents of strategies other than those employed. In any case, simple annual samplings by the Census Bureau would indicate progress or no progress and good progress or poor progress utilizing 1970 census figures as a baseline.

The goals are flexible and arrived at through application of value standards. Bachelor's degrees for 20 percent of the twenty-four-to-twenty-nine-year-old group are based on labor-force projections of needs for college-trained people and the prognosis of economists that 20 percent of the jobs in the labor force will require a degree. If this prognosis shows an increase, so should the goals for producing black college graduates. The goal of twenty thousand physicians could be higher but such a goal is realistic. The attainment of this goal will require tripling the number of minorities in a setup that has places for only eighteen thousand new students a year and receives applications from three students for every place. The 100 percent graduation rate may be high by 10 percent, but new forms of certification of experiences added to high-school and GED certification may make high-school graduation truly universal.

Finally, the goals and time frames offer good measuring sticks for both school administrators and community groups bedeviled by uncertainty of school progress. If high-school graduation rates are inching up one or two percentage points a year with one-half the graduating classes going off to college and one-half of this group picking up a degree, the school system is moving forward where blacks are concerned.

Black and white colleges may also measure their performance

in this manner. Some already do. Morehouse College, a black school in Atlanta, for example, has a goal of producing more Ph.D. recipients per capita than any school in Georgia regardless of race. The school has maintained a commanding lead for the past twenty-five years. Southern University in Baton Rouge set similar goals for Ph.D.'s in the biological sciences and is able to come up with a good report each year.

Continuing education may be the most difficult area in which to measure progress while being one of the more important forms of education to blacks. As mentioned earlier, blacks will have to depend on this type of education quite heavily, and both races will have to use it far more heavily in the future than in the past.

A worthy beginning study would be a comprehensive analysis of black participation in continuing education. Nearly 250,000 persons received GED diplomas in 1971 but no racial breakdown is available. Job Corps and apprentice figures are available for blacks, but for each enrollee, there are probably three enrollees each in military, industrial, or proprietary schools, plus perhaps twice this number in general adult-education programs.

Again, clear goals and time frames can be quite beneficial in the drive for quality education for black Americans. The frames can reduce frustration and bickering and increase motivation and effort by presenting a clear idea of where the drive is headed and periodic read-outs of progress toward these goals.

Choosing the Right Weapons

At this point the strategies of school and government begin to come apart. Many manage to confuse process evaluation with product evaluation. Others succumb to the temptations to pull up programs by their roots to see if they are growing. Most have no comprehensive strategies to bring schooling from point A to point B. Many Washington movers wear proudly the nom de plume of "change agents." School administrators vie in the newspaper as "innovators," changing and innovating for what is all too often unclear.

Effective evaluation of progress in the drive to quality education for black Americans will require (1) a good grasp of overall goals by every local school district involved, (2) an understanding of efforts to make annual audits of progress, (3) a good grasp of local progress toward goals, and (4) the expertise to develop annual audits toward these goals.

Many states and school districts are far from developing these insights and competencies. The author has held earnest discussion with men and women to whom funds and responsibility have been given to improve the schooling of blacks. Most responsible educators cannot state correctly the black population of America or of their school units. Virtually none can state accurate figures on black graduation rates, nationally or locally. These educators can not speak authoritatively on black college attendance, production of black professionals, or any other aspect of black life and culture. Add to this a news writer or two with knowledge of measurement of school programs that is limited to age-grade equivalents on tests and a confusing situation evolves to say the least.

Effective Process Evaluation

Given the goals stated above and others that may be added, government and school administrators simply need to develop means of assessing which combinations of factors are moving them toward their goals at a satisfactory pace. The key phrase is *movement toward goals at a satisfactory pace.* Many school programs have become little more than wasted money and motion because either clear goals were not set or goals were unrealistic. Other programs have become a can of worms because good programs were eliminated in favor of something that promised to be quicker. George Weber of the Council for Basic Education, for example, identified ninety-five schools succeeding with black children in depressed areas, selected four, and studied them carefully for a year. He identified strong administrators, high teacher expectations, strong phonics teaching, and frequent progress testing as key elements in schools making satisfactory progress toward goals. This conventional approach is too mundane, too pedestrian for most school "innovators," however. The innovators think: "Why, it is very much like we were taught. Surely something else more exotic must be put forward. How can extra funding be justified for strong administration, strong phonics, high teacher expectations, and frequent progress testing? How can we generate papers for the annual meetings and have topics for theses and dissertations?" The black child really is often adrift on the sea of schemes and exotic programs about which Andrew Brimmer complains. The absence on the part of his mentors of clear realistic goals and the impulses toward exotic programs promising rapid results serve to do little for the child.

Given clear goals, however, or driven by government and community to define these goals, school administrators can install a basic program and begin to evaluate it in the context of these goals or they can evaluate the present program. Regardless, the goals of high-school graduation, college attendance, production of professionals and lifelong continuing education are the contexts in which processes must be evaluated.

Local baseline data are first and necessary steps. What is the graduate rate? Has it been rising or falling during the past five years? At what rate? What are critical grade or age levels affecting graduation rates? These are simple data, but a safe bet is that most school districts enrolling blacks do not have the answers.

Parsed-factor data must then be developed. What components of the school experience seem important in persistence and attrition? College attendance? Enrollment in professional schools? Lifelong continuing education? These questions require sophisticated research, but many firms can complete it for a nominal fee. Further, once identified in a number of districts in a region, other districts can borrow the findings and eliminate the need for studies of their own.

Parsed factors, probably resulting from stepwise regression

analysis, will be varied. Persistence in school, for example, might be shown to be enhanced by schools that make children feel very good about themselves, are self-pacing, have teachers with keen insights and kind dispositions, teach phonics strongly, put the poorest children in age three to five pre-K and the very poorest in age birth to three cradle schools, use locator-criterion testing, and arrange for work-study programs for adolescents.

The key is the participation of the district itself in reviewing its goals and parsing out those factors enabling children to reach them. Each district needs this experience, even if studies of parsed factors are borrowed from other districts.

The government used parsed-factor data in analyzing economic gains of blacks. A study of such gains by the Conference Board (an independent business research group), for example, revealed the sort of facts needed for policy development in both educational and economic areas.[1] The Conference Board found that between 1965 and 1970 black income grew 60 per cent, while white income grew 40 per cent. Planners must aim for this sort of overgain in the drive to eliminate gaps. Further, analysis by the Conference Board revealed that one-half the gain came in 1966, the first full year of operation of the Equal Employment Opportunity Commission. For the first time, the impact of a weapon on strategy had been assessed. In short, the drive toward the clear goal (the product) of comparability in income bore fruit in the past five years, and the strategies of enforcing equal opportunity laws (the process) has emerged as an effective approach.

A corollary in a school district might be the study of overgains in black graduation rates and pegging the initiation of a work-study program as a key factor. Black college enrollment took a big jump, for example, with the initiation of equal opportunity scholarships by the government.

Process Evaluation and Testing

The point at which process evaluation is likely to founder is in the testing arena. A limited knowledge of the dynamics of normative testing is likely to be a key factor. Many superintendents will find themselves cringing before an all-seeing, all-knowing research bureau in their own shops and "hot media" representatives to which test scores can be released. Careful planning can enable school people to avoid this trouble.

First, the end-of-year school testing must be eliminated for most of the children. These tests are the sources of most of the difficulty and all the chief sources of injurious child-racing (my child is two points higher than yours).

Second, locator and criterion testing is installed with clear goals for the children and clear methods of assessing progress toward these goals. Instead of stating that the "child will read at the third grade level," the district spells out reading competencies it is shooting for with a time frame (short-term products). Criterion tests can then assess the children's progress toward these goals.

The Maryland Task Force on Reading Competence has come up with good examples of this approach.[2] This group has set five objectives in reading for graduates of Maryland schools and developed a method of assessing progress toward these objectives.

The task force (a state department of education group) sets the following goals and subcategories for the children:

1. Following Directions
   a. using directional vocabularies
   b. understanding sequential-order directions
   c. understanding cautions, warnings, and labels
   d. finding locations
2. Locating References
   a. using single sources
   b. using multivolume sources
   c. using multiresource centers
3. Attaining Personal Development
   a. reading for personal satisfaction
   b. reading for entertainment
   c. reading as adjuncts to other personal goals and pursuits

4. Gaining Information
   a. for school and college work
   b. for vocational choices and vocational development
   c. for ordering personal and legal affairs
5. Understanding Forms
   a. personal and legal
   b. financial agreements
   c. government forms

The Maryland child who reaches these objectives will be quite proficient indeed. The task force spells out some eighty to eighty-five exemplars of reading skill it wishes its graduates to master.

Under *Following Directions,* for example, the task force wants the students to be able to handle:

Road signs	Mechanical device directions
Building signs	Voting machines
Textbook instructions	Child-care material
Emergency signs	First-aid directions
Trade directions	Survival signs
Games	Labels
Do-it-yourself kits	Local community street signs
Cooking recipes	Work schedules
Sewing patterns	Maps

The competent Marylander will be able to handle the following resources for locating information:

Consumer's Guide	Textbook
T.V. Guide	Tradebook
Encyclopedia	Job manual
Reader's Guide	Dictionary
Index volume	Newspaper
Atlases	Magazine
Library card catalogue	Almanac
Reference books	Phone book
and materials	
Section titles	Catalogue

To gain information the graduate will delve and rummage proficiently through:

Public announcements	Basic prescribed essential
Company policy statements	vocabulary lists
Union contracts	Assignments
Legal documents	Training manuals
Emergency announcements	Safety and job requirements
Newspaper materials	Memoranda
Work schedules	Want ads

And the following forms will pose little difficulty:

Mail-order purchase forms	Social security forms
Credit-card applications	Medical forms
Bank statements	Applications
Notes and loans	Armed forces
Sales and rent agreements	Sales slips
School forms	Subscriptions
Tax forms	Hotel reservations
Insurance forms	Long-term contracts

Test items geared to these goals are used in the Maryland scheme. Reading objectives have been spelled out in great detail and items developed for each objective. Objective 5201 (a code), for example, is related to category five above. The objective states that "students will be able to read and translate financial agreements." Test items for 5201 are as follows:

John has decided to join the Citadel Record Club. If he sends in the coupon below he will receive
  (a) a cassette tape
  (b) eleven records
  (c) a Gold Medal Award
  (d) twenty-two records
After John buys twelve records at member's prices, he can buy
  (a) ten records for $1.87
  (b) eight tapes and one record

(c) two records for the price of one

(d) two cassettes for the price of one

A sales agreement for the record company is included as part of the test.

Objective 2101 states that "students will be able to read to locate information by utilizing the table of contents, index, glossary, appendix, footnotes, bibliography, and headings."

Test items for 2101 are as follows:

Tom is preparing a report on the bad effects of smoking. On what page of this magazine could he find information to add to his report?

(a) 101   (c) 84

(b) 56   (d) 61

Mary has to write a review of a play for her school newspaper. To get an idea of what to include in a review, she should look on page

(a) 58   (c) 56

(b) 18   (d) 88

A condensed table of contents of a magazine is included in the test.

Time frames are carefully spelled out in the Maryland operation. Most indicate an age span of twelve to eighteen years of age. This time frame leaves the primary years of school as a skills-building period that can be devoted to phonics, comprehension, and facility. Locator and criterion tests are included in most reading programs for these skills. Timewise, Maryland aims for textbook direction understanding at age twelve with increased facility up to age eighteen. Voting and child-care directions are postponed until age eighteen. Footnotes and bibliographic skills begin at age twelve, but subscription forms are begun at age fifteen.

Reporting results in criterion evaluation eliminate many problems. The report does not have to state that the children scrambled to a mark quicker or slower than a national norm group. The report simply has to set forth a listing of objectives in reading, the time frames, and the number of students who reached the objective. For example:

Objective	Time Frame	Student Performance
Reading to follow sequential directions for first aid	15–18 yrs.	1025/25

The report is direct. No mystery surrounds the contents of a test or what the norm group did or of whom they were composed or even about the number involved in the district, which is so often camouflaged by percentages. Citizens and teachers know that within a three-year period, most district students have developed skills in reading and following directions for first aid and that a small number did not and must develop this skill, perhaps, through continuing education.

To make a comprehensive report to the public, the district would present an analysis of objectives reached by reading categories. For example:

Categories	Number of Objectives	Number Reached
Reading for direction	15	80% of children 70% of children

The report then goes on to identify highly successful areas and areas needing improvement.

The public, as well as the teachers and administrators, has a complete understanding of what the teachers are trying to do and the extent to which they are reaching their goals. This clarity is simply unavailable in many of today's test reports. Steelworkers and accountants are simply left blank when given a report showing that the district's children scored at the fifty-second percentile on a reading test that measured some unclear factors. Many teachers are similarly affected. If statistical gymnastics such as standard deviations are added to the report, a sense of distrust sets in.

Problems of the Competitive Spirit

Although the cultural ethos in America is turning toward a mature concept of cooperative endeavor within which unique individual approaches and structures are given the highest priority, district leaders will continue to be plagued with problems of test competition in the years ahead.

The psychometrists within the system are trained in normative-based testing and will wish to keep on doing what they are doing—sorting and racing children. Then, certain parents build their entire life around the development of a "bright" child, one who is many percentiles above the norm. Unlike others in this scenario, these parents are more to be pitied than despised. Some parents use their children to compensate for the aches and pains of their own childhoods or the emptiness of their present lives. Still other parents are simply overly competitive and race their children like they race everything else in their lives, their house, their manservants. Finally, some people and groups use both bad and good test scores as power levers. These people include ideologues from the press and other sectors, community groups, and politicians.

American education has not always been in a position where something that was designed by the schools to help children can be twisted in such a way as to hurt them. When Alfred Binet invented the first tests a scant seventy years ago, he was trying with every fiber to help children. For a while he succeeded in keeping his tests to simple locator instruments designed to find out where children were and what sort of instruction would help them grow. Much later, misadvised individuals developed age-grade norms, IQ tests, and other instruments enabling children to be placed into highly competitive positions. The situation has deteriorated so rapidly in the last twenty-five years that some New York parents spend large sums of money to have their children tested for practice in hopes of getting them into the "right" nursery schools, then the "right" kindergarten, the "right" elementary and prep schools, and finally the "right" college. Is it any wonder that one New England university maintains a cadre of sixteen psychiatrists? The only power to reform this situation rests with schoolteachers and administrators and teacher-training institutions.

A good place to start this reform is at the local level in test reporting on student progress. For parents who want to know how their child is doing in reading, teachers simply have to give or send a list of reading objectives with an indication of those reached by the child. Teachers are tempted to send the date completed but are faced with the problem of parents seeing these dates and comparing them with other parents and the child race is on again.

Simple numerical reporting of objectives reached can also be made to competition-hungry ideologues, and sophisticated analysis of test scores can bear fruit.

The report may point out, for example, that children from working-class families who were headed toward careers in crafts and technology had done exceptionally well in reaching objectives related to these areas and that they had done a creditable job in reaching objectives less relevant to the roads they are traveling. In this respect working-class children, headed toward college or a life of letters, were doing well in these objectives and were doing a creditable job in handling crafts and technology material.

Finally, reports may point out that children of professional families, who were headed toward crafts and technology, were doing well in this material, and hopefully, more professional parents were allowing and sometimes encouraging their children to do this. Crafts and technology children were able to prepare for college participation with a change in program and extra study, and many college-bound students switched into crafts and technology.

Measurement and reporting are the biggest obstacles to effective instruction and the operation of a good school system. Educators who wish to have a good program must first wrestle with this devil. The crafts-technology/college-bound dichotomy is analogous to C. P. Snow's *Two Cultures*. Children are set on career roads by families and learn what is necessary for success in these careers. Sometimes in the case of college-bound children, the material is archaic and meaningless but it is learned in the name of preservation and transmission of the culture. The craft and technology child must also learn the mysteries of his guilds and the life that awaits him. The college-bound material may interest the craft and technology child to some extent. If proficiency and skill in diemaking are his goals in life however, he must devote his full attention to material in this arena.

This dynamic accounts for the differences in test scores in various communities when other factors are fairly even. Educators have never been able or willing to explain this dynamic to the public or to themselves. The result is an unusual amount of hand wringing and attacks on both the schools and working-class families by intellectuals who seem to feel that regardless of life-styles and careers everyone should learn and test out well on a curriculum designed to prepare children for entrance into the Princeton freshman class of 1935.

Careful comprehensive reporting of sophisticated analyses of how the children are progressing in their schooling will lessen the acrimony surrounding what can only be described as a bad testing and reporting apparatus. Everybody from the President of the United States to cradle-school teachers has a responsibility to insist that this reporting is done.

Annual Education-Economic Audits

The schools of a community are expected to be the ladders by which people clamber up the economic scale into comfortable lives and the mechanisms through which people can keep from tumbling back down again (if you lose your job, go back to school). Communities expect schools to perform for their children as they did for them and perhaps improve on this performance. As noted in the first chapter of this book, much of this belief is based on myth and legend. A combination of good education and good economic opportunity did improve the lives of many people in the past, and many EE (education-economic) tandems are helping blacks today.

An annual EE audit of community, state, and national efforts to offer quality education to black children and youth would seem beneficial. The audit would be instructive to many whites who have no idea of what is transpiring in this area. Some whites have the idea that no progress is being made. Others feel that so much progress is being made that they must complain of favoritism and preferential treatment. Some blacks and whites have little idea of what is a good index of progress. Then, one group finds grasping the intricacies of test descriptions hard. The Niagara Falls stalwart who trumpeted that the trouble with the schools is that "65 percent of the kids ain't learning reading and the other 45 percent can't do arithmetic" is representative of the mentality of many who take a dim view of things.

What should be reported in such an audit? What indices of progress can be used? What indices of regression are to be used?

Statements of progress of the children toward learning objectives is surely data that must be included. Excellent indices are data showing increases in the number of children staying in school, increases in average daily attendance, increases in numbers continuing their education in various ways, and increases in the continuing-education program of the district.

Increases in the number of blacks in skilled and well-paying jobs in crafts and technology and the professions can be included in the audit. The schools helped generate much of this advanced reporting. All children who have excelled in their school activities in any way at all must be included. First, those children who worked hard and reached many learning objectives must be acclaimed. This number will include crafts-technology children as well as the usual awards to college-bound children. Then, bouquets will go to students who sculpted, painted, ran, jumped, presided, led, organized, cooperated, experimented, and acted well, just to name a few of the many possible rewards.

Finally, one must report on the children's perceptions of their school experiences. Are they rewarding, helpful, supportive? Do the students feel better or worse about themselves after being exposed to these experiences? Do the alumni look back in fondness and appreciation of their experience? Figure 18 is a hypothetical example of an annual school audit that

FIGURE 18
CROSS CITY SCHOOLS
QUALITY EDUCATION PROGRAM *—ANNUAL AUDIT
1972

Item	1971 Performance	1972 Performance	+ — Change
Average Daily Attendance	90%	92%	+2
High-School Graduation (of fifth-grade base group)	70%	71%	+1
Percentage of Former Students in Further Study: Graduates	60%	65%	+5
Students Changing Form of Education **	10%	8%	−2
Enrollment of Changers in GED-Type Programs	70%	80%	+10
Enrollment of Graduates in Apprentice Programs	10%	12%	+2
College Scholarship and Awards (of students enrolling)	70%	80%	+10
Completion of Reading Objectives (12-year-olds)	2000/150	2000/150	——***
		(of 2,150 12-year-olds, 2000 had completed reading objectives targeted for this age level and 150 were still working on them)	
Completion of Reading Objectives (15-year-olds)	1910/120	1935/100	——
Completion of Reading Objectives (18-year-olds)	1735/106	1750/110	——
Citations for Exemplary Students (total school population)	45%	50%	+5
Exemplary Work to Complete Learning Objectives	25%	30%	+5
Art and Music	14%	15%	+1
Science	9%	10%	+1
Athletics	19%	20%	+1
Alumni Continuing Their Education (Includes College and Adult Education)	75%	80%	+5
Alumni in Profession-Crafts-Technology Jobs	45%	50%	+5
School Organizations and Activities	38%	40%	+2

FIGURE 18 (Continued)
CROSS CITY SCHOOLS
QUALITY EDUCATION PROGRAM *—ANNUAL AUDIT
1972

Item	1971 Performance	1972 Performance	+ − Change
Score Alumni School Per- ceptions Index	75%	80%	+5
		(100 equals perfect score)	

* The Quality Education Program is designed specifically for minority students (mostly black) in our district.
** Formerly but no longer alluded to as dropouts.
*** Change is not reported here in the interest of minimizing the competitive spirit.

might appear in a newspaper in a school district dedicated to quality education for black Americans.

This report can be embellished in many ways, but even an untrained observer can readily understand that Cross City Schools are dedicated to and deeply involved in the cause of equal opportunity through quality education. The schools together with equal opportunity employers, lenders, and industrial representatives who do business with blacks are succeeding in Cross City. The youngsters are staying in school instead of leaving early. Those young people who leave are entering programs leading to a GED certificate. The unions are recruiting the youngsters for apprentice programs. The guidance officers are doing yeoman's service in getting black students financial aid for college. The instructional objectives are clear and the children are reaching them. No hysteria surrounds those who need extra time.

The children are working hard in school and winning citations for their good work in a variety of fields. The alumni are geared up for lifelong education, are getting good jobs, and will raise even healthier and brighter children. The alumni feel that the school is owed a debt of gratitude for its work in getting them into a better station in life or for preparing them to maintain the good situations they already had. The people of Cross City feel good about their schools. The business and industrial community is keenly aware of the necessity of adequate family incomes in order for children to do well in school. Businessmen and industrialists are working hard to make equal opportunity a reality at all levels in their operations. The people know what to expect of their schools and how to evaluate school efforts. The constructive social energies of many people are harnessed productively in the school program. Clear goals are in sight. Bench marks of progress are clear to all. A critical mass of resources is being applied.

Notes for Chapter 8

[1] Virginian Pilot, April 22, 1972, p. A–11.

[2] *Report of the Maryland Task Force on Reading Competence.* Mimeographed. Maryland Department of Education, 1972.

Epilogue

A CELEBRATION of a decade or so of progress in education for black Americans, an analysis of present needs for improvement, and a projection of ways and means of bringing about these improvements have been the thrusts of the foregoing pages. Much has been done in the drive toward excellence for a greater proportion of black children and youth and much yet remains to be done. Society changes and education must change too. The challenge of excellence is always with us.

The programs suggested here are surely a challenge to Americans everywhere and a special challenge to people of good will who work diligently to perfect the country in the image of those who dreamed of a more perfect society. Planners are urged to link progress in education more closely to economic progress for minorities in the interest of synergism and common sense. Test abuse and the subsequent malsorting of poor black children must receive a high order in any set of priorities. Middle-class black children must receive a higher quality of education than some integrated schools now afford. Integrated schools without truly integrated administrative staffs and faculties are not quality schools. The bald fact of the matter is that these schools are counterproductive and do serious damage to the very students the black community must depend on to provide most of its leadership and professional and technical workers. All school integration is not good and more and more people must face up to this fact.

Poor black children can now benefit from excellent high-impact programs to enable them to learn more efficiently, but school planners and administrators must be persuaded to use the programs and faculties must bend every oar to make them work. Much of the school leadership is committed to either increasing the amount of time and effort expended on old ineffective programs or experimenting with untried and patently unworkable schemes to improve teaching and learning. This is more and more untenable as successes with high-impact programs continue to pile up.

The most glaring imbalances in the quality of education can be found in the numbers of black children receiving their education in vocational and special-education programs. Both programs bring up the rear in any parade of excellence, and any program to improve the quality of schooling of black children and youth must include a strenuous effort to correct this imbalance in enrollment while improving the programs themselves for the students who remain in them. Excellent school-business-industry programs are operating for vocational students but they are not widespread. More and more children are being "mainstreamed" out of special-education programs. These numbers must be increased further through petitions, court actions, and legislation to correct the test abuses that assign minority children unfairly to these classes.

Black and white youth and adults must more and more depend on continuing education to complete interrupted schooling, to use as a substitute for schooling of low quality, and to keep abreast of education demands in a rapidly changing work force. Continuing education is perhaps the best conceived and executed program in education today. It allows us to inter the unfortunate term *school dropout* in favor of the phrase *changing the form of schooling*. It combines earning and learning in many cases and uses a wide variety of very effective teaching strategies and materials. Blacks and whites must join forces to avail themselves more widely of these benefits.

A new breed of metropolitan college is coming onto the scene, and if developed widely and rapidly, this institution could be of vast assistance to metropolitan dwellers of all hues and particularly to black Americans. Blacks are in the curious position of making striking progress in college enrollment while still falling behind a white society that seems intent on sending every eighteen-year-old to college whether he wants to go or not. With the demise of the draft and a glutted job market, the drive toward "universal higher education" has slowed and new metropolitan colleges will enable the black community to carefully assess its manpower and service needs and use these colleges to meet them.

The drive to educate poor children more thoroughly has, predictably, caused some reactionaries to begin to gnaw once again at the bones of the nature-nurture debate. Predictably, too, racists have made one final stand (a death rattle it seems) on the battlefield of white and Aryan supremacy. They have been given short shrift and time must not be wasted on their thoughts. The record is speaking for itself. Mistakes are made in planning, however, and must be lessened and hopefully eliminated. The various government programs, as a single example, have yet to call for the use of accurate tests in their thousands of programs for minority children.

It is entirely possible to look to the year 2000 as a time when imbalance in both the quality and the quantity of education black Americans receive will be a rapidly fading memory, but a government-school-industry partnership will be necessary to bring this about and serious work on the part of the black community will also be demanded.

True equality of opportunity in the marketplace must become a reality. Successful young blacks must be living carrots to those who come behind. Metropolitan job banks operated at government expense must take up the slack wherever it exists in placing the new high-school graduates. Federal funds for schooling from cradle schools to graduate fellowships must judiciously buttress state and local efforts where needed.

Gifted black children and youth must receive more attention. This is especially true in depressed communties. School programs must be expanded in this area and the black community must increase its efforts to stretch these young minds. Excellent programs are under way in some communities. They must be expanded to many more.

A fine effort will be required on many fronts in the years ahead in the drive for quality education. But improvements of the order described are entirely within the capabilities of the American people. If the old Freedmen's Bureau had not been abolished and if the beginnings of equal access to jobs, business opportunities, and schooling of that time had not withered on the vine, our job would be done by now. It will be sad indeed if workers in these vineyards must say in 1999 that if the fine progress of the sixties and seventies had been continued and accelerated, *their* job would be completed. There is no logical reason at all why this should happen, and it will be yet another blight on the record of morality of Americans if it should. Quality education for black Americans is completely within our grasp. Hard work and dedication to the principle will bring it about.

Appendices

EXEMPLARY PROGRAMS

A—*Cradle Schools*

B—*Early Education*

C—*Elementary Education*

D—*Reading Improvement*

E—*High-School Work-Study Programs*

F—*Legislation to Curb Test Abuse*

Cradle Schools

Exemplary Programs: Cradle Schools

Program: Milwaukee Cradle Schools *

Location: Milwaukee, Wisconsin

Population Served: About sixty children ages five days to five years

Description:

In 1966, the Infant Education Center was established in the slum area of Milwaukee where original surveys documenting poverty were conducted.

Three elements were considered essential for the success of the center.

First, the project had to improve the welfare of the *entire family*. The mothers were offered on-the-job occupational training and instruction in homemaking and child care.

Second, a program of instruction was carefully planned and structured. A curriculum from birth to age six was carefully programmed before the children were born.

And third, teaching started almost from birth. Rather than waiting until the child was already lagging behind others, the project aimed at preventing any intellectual stagnation.

Shortly after the mothers returned home from the maternity

---

* Excerpted from "Learn, Baby, Learn," by Clifford C. Marcussen and John Kilburn, The Plain Truth (March–April, 1972), pp. 23–27.

ward of the hospital, teachers began visiting them to spend several hours a day playing with and talking to the babies.

After three to six months and when both mother and teacher agreed that the time was right—the infant began spending part of each day at the Infant Education Center.

Until age two, each infant had a personal teacher. The teachers continued to play with the babies, exposing them to a wide variety of mentally stimulating games, sights, and sounds. The biggest goal during this period was to build the child's *understanding of words*—long before he began to speak. As the children reached age two, they began small-group learning. Two or three teachers were assigned to each group of five to ten children. Thus, individualized attention was maintained.

Today, the children range in ages from 3 to 5 years. They are bright, motivated, talkative, and active.

Monday through Friday, the children spend seven hours a day at the Center. Each child attends five "classes" a day, covering three subjects—language, reading, and math problem-solving.

Breakfast, lunch, a snack, nap time, and free play fill the rest of the day. Thursdays are often set aside for field trips to the beach, a pumpkin farm, the airport, a bread factory, a ranch or just a walk around the block to look at the trees and collect leaves.

The result?

It would be difficult to find a group of preschool children more genuinely interested and excited in learning. The children love to hear stories or make up their own. Sometimes they even play "teacher."

They talk freely among themselves or with the teachers. Although they can speak the dialect of English common to their slum they can also speak clear and correct schoolroom English. After hearing a visitor from Washington remark, "Ain't this a fine morning," one child told the guest, "That isn't the right way to say that."

Last November, the "slowest" of the five-year-olds had a sight-reading vocabulary of twenty words. The four-year-olds could identify well over eight basic colors and the basic geometric shapes. They are now mastering such games as picking out a red square from a blue square and a red triangle.

In short, the children are performing tasks a year or more ahead of "normal" children.

The Wisconsin researchers have carefully monitored the children's intelligence progress with the standard Stanford-Binet Intelligence Test, and the children have absolutely astounded their teachers.

Without their special schooling these children would be starting to show signs of mental retardation. They now had an *average* I.Q. of 120. As a group, they were in the top 10% of the nation. Scores ranged from a low of 100 (which is the national average) to a high of 135 (well within the "gifted" category).

The children have also done extremely well on over 20 other tests of learning and language. A team of experts who analyzed their production and comprehension of language rated them as "superior."

According to Dr. Heber, "We have seen a capacity for learning on the part of extremely young children, surpassing anything which I would have previously believed possible." It is difficult, he has written, to conceive of the children as ever falling back to the level of comparable slum children.

The children have demonstrated conclusively that progressive mental retardation can be prevented.

Early Education

Exemplary Programs: Early Education

Project Title: Home Start II *

Location: Waterloo, Iowa

Population Served: 171 two-year-old children

Project Motivation:

Children from disadvantaged families too often enter school with gaps in experience, which, left unidentified and uncorrected, cause initial failure and future underachievement. To eliminate such gaps, parental attitudes and behavior must be modified to create a home environment conducive to learning. A program of home visits by trained staff serves the dual purpose of educating parents and monitoring parent-child interaction.

Description:

Home Start is a three-year program that guides a child and his parent(s) through two years of home enrichment, followed by a 2½-hour classroom experience five days a week in the prekindergarten year. During this third year, the focus continues to be on facilitating learning within the home; in the project, educational procedures are being individualized, using results from the LRS Seriation Test.

---

* This program was selected by the U.S. Office of Education for display at its 1972 Education Fair.

Throughout the three-year period, an achievement-oriented test is administered at six-month intervals to enable the home visitor to individualize educational procedures employed within the home. Paid aides and staff members (speech consultant, home economist, and so forth, depending upon need) visit homes to improve parent-child interaction, including the selection of educational toys for stimulating development within the home. Mothers come to the Home Start Center to pick up instructional materials. Three consultants work with the mothers to aid them in teaching their children. Various community agencies also work with the project to provide services for the children and families of both groups.

Major Resources Required for Implementation:

The cost of installing the Home Start II model for 170–175 children is about $130,000; second-year costs should remain approximately the same. Estimates are that costs will rise an extra $30,000 in the third year to include two teachers, two full-time aides, and the service of two buses needed to transport children to and from their class.

Result: Two types of data were obtained from evaluations: (1) the first-grade Primary Mental Abilities (PMA) test scores from children in the same attendance area, and (2) PMA scores for older siblings who had not participated in the program. Black Home Start children scored 100.9 on the PMA, while non-project children scored 95.0. They outscored their siblings 100.9 to 93.5. The project directors recognize the inadequacies of the PMA because of cultural biases but note that black Home Start children exceeded the average on the test.

Exemplary Programs: Early Education

Project Title: Child-Parent Centers
Location: Chicago, Illinois
Population Served: 2,100 children ages three through nine

Description:

The Child-Parent Centers (CPC), funded through ESEA Title I, are administered by the Chicago Board of Education in areas characterized by a high density of low-income families. Approximately 2,100 children, ages three through nine, are enrolled in the eleven centers, which offer up to six years of education including two years of preschool education, kindergarten, and primary grades one to three.

The instructional program at each of the eleven centers is highly basic skills oriented, with an emphasis on language development, so that pupils become more successful readers. Approaches and instructional materials are selected or developed by the local center staff working cooperatively with the Parent Advisory Council.

Supporting the instructional program at all centers is a nutrition and health program. The practical nurse, the teacher-nurse, and the teacher-social worker all participate to a degree in the early identification of pupil health problems, in helping parents recognize problems that may need medical attention, and in arranging referral and follow-up services for pupils and their parents.

The parent program is a major factor contributing to the success of the Child-Parent Centers. Some parents serve regularly in the classroom, others create material for the classroom, still others meet in a small group with a teacher to learn how to instruct their own children at home. Typical involvements include typewriting classes, GED classes, Spanish-English classes, home cooperatives, fashion shows, and fund-raising events.

Each center has a school-community representative, a home economist for parents, the services of a teacher-nurse and a teacher-social worker—all of whom work closely with the parents. Staff members also visit the families in their homes.

The annual per pupil expenditure for a CPC student is

$1,447 * (cost includes a six-week summer program), compared to the city-wide expenditure of $1,114.

The CPC program incorporates the key features of both Headstart and Follow Through, as well as Home Start, which emphasizes parent education. The CPC approach and program are also highly consistent with the most recent research and evaluation studies.

Seven years of CPC experiences have demonstrated that the early start, structured curricula, and parental involvement work and also have a ripple effect in the community. CPC children score *above* national norms on readiness tests and on achievement tests in all grades. CPC "graduates" hold their own and better in middle and junior high schools.

---

* This figure includes $1,237 in federal monies and $210 in local contributions.

Elementary Education

Exemplary Program: Elementary Education

Program: The Woodland Street School *

Location: Kansas City, Missouri

Population Served: 650 children

Description:

There are about 650 pupils in kindergarten through seventh grade at Woodland Street School. Before urban renewal demolished so many buildings, there had been 1,200 pupils. Ninety-nine percent of the children are black; almost all of them are very poor. About 90 percent get free or largely free lunch.

Last school year (1970–71) was the second year as principal for Don Joslin. Previously he had been principal of another Title I school. Mr. Joslin believes in the power of cooperation, and he often deals with pupils in terms of asking them for "help."

Classes are relatively large. Last spring each of the three regular third-grade classes (one was a combined class of third- and fourth-graders) had 29 pupils. A special education class for second- and third-graders had 14. Including that class, the pupil-teacher ratio for the third grade was 25.3:1.

---

* This description is reprinted from George Weber, *Inner City Children Can Be Taught to Read* (Council for Basic Education, Washington, D.C., 1971).

Woodland School is part of a multi-school program, Project Uplift. The driving force behind this project is a black man, Robert R. Wheeler,* area superintendent for the Division of Urban Education. Mr. Wheeler served with the Kansas City schools before he went to Oakland, California, for three years. When he returned to Kansas City in 1966, he was determined to improve the reading achievement of children in the inner city. "We began," he has said, "with the fundamental belief that inner-city pupils can learn as well as other pupils, provided the priorities are sensible, the effort intense, and the instructional approaches rational in terms of the needs of the learners. We have not accepted the myth that environmental factors develop unalterable learning depression. We believe that so-called negative environmental factors can be overcome with sensitive and responsive teaching." In the fall of 1968, when the educational establishment was contending that slum children were permanently disadvantaged and, in Mr. Wheeler's words, "needed more zoo trips or didn't have enough oatmeal," he began a program that emphasized beginning reading skills.

The program included reading and speech specialists in each school, teacher aides, and a change from traditional whole-word basals to the Sullivan Programmed Reading Series. In-service training of teachers was crucial because staff expectations about pupil potential had to be raised. As Mr. Wheeler put it, "The staff has to believe the pupils can and will learn before they can convince the students that they are not doomed to fail."

The Sullivan program has built into it a regular procedure of individual evaluation, the page and end-of-book checks. Even if this is implemented with only moderate competence, the resulting reading evaluation system is far superior to that typically carried out in the primary classes of our public schools.

Woodland, like other Project Uplift schools, has a full-time "speech improvement" teacher. She spends 20 to 25 minutes twice a week in each of the classes from kindergarten through fourth grade. She uses a variety of techniques, including chil-

---

* Dr. Wheeler is now serving as Associate Commissioner for Elementary and Secondary Education in the U.S. Office of Education.

dren's plays and oral reports to class, to improve pupils' verbal facility so that youngsters can move from the neighborhood dialect to the English used in the classroom.

The school has two full-time reading specialists, one of whom is assigned to kindergarten through grade three, the other to grades four through seven. These specialists do not teach the children outside of the classroom. Their duties include in-service work with the classroom teachers, demonstrations in the classroom, and general monitoring of the reading program.

The school has a library which children visit once a week. They may borrow books to take back to use in the classroom, but they may not take books home.

Woodland has a state-aided program of special education. There are three classes: one for second and third grades, one for fourth and fifth, and one for sixth and seventh. Assignment to the classes is made on the basis of a Stanford-Binet score of 79 IQ or lower. Children are assigned to the classes for three years at a time and cannot be retested for possible reassignment to regular classes during that period. Last spring 12 third-graders were assigned to the special education class. Although the children had worked in the Sullivan series when they were in the regular classes, in the special education class they used a whole-word basal series. Out of the ten tested third-graders who were non-readers, seven were in the special education class.

The most important factors in Woodland's success in beginning reading instruction are the high expectations and the use of the McGraw-Hill Sullivan program. The considerable time devoted to reading is another factor. The reading and speech specialists and the teacher aides round out the picture. The special education classes are probably, on balance, a negative factor.

Reading Improvement

Exemplary Programs: Reading Improvement

Project Title: Urban Education Reading Program *

Location: Kansas City, Missouri

Population Served: Currently serving 7,498 educationally disadvantaged children in eighteen elementary and four secondary target schools

Project Motivation: The Kansas City, Missouri, Division of Urban Education was organized in July, 1966, and charged with the responsibility for developing and implementing educational programs specifically designed to meet the specialized needs of inner-city children. Educational needs were determined by the administration of standardized tests. The highest concentration of need was found to be in the area of reading and language arts. Subsequently, a developmental and corrective reading program was designed and geared to the specialized needs of the learner.

Description: The reading program is an individualized instructional approach designed to raise the achievement level in reading of project participants by six to nine months during nine months of instruction and to improve the pupil's ability to communicate through learning, speaking, and writing about meaningful, real-life experiences. A reading specialist in each school

---

* This program was selected by the U.S. Office of Education for display at its 1972 Education Fair.

assists teachers and principals in planning reading programs and in developing teaching techniques appropriate for meeting the individual pupil needs. The reading specialist assists classroom teachers in developing daily reading instructional materials and providing corrective or remedial instruction to pupils in small groups. Programmed reading textbooks are used as the main teaching aid. These textbooks are supplemented by a variety of reading activities, books, and other materials.

To stimulate effective communication and speech improvement, special emphasis is given to phonetics and to auditory training, which supports and reinforces the programmed reading.

Paraprofessionals (many of whom are parents) are employed as teacher aides and as secretaries, thus enabling the teacher to utilize her professional skills to the maximum.

Parents and school staff work as a team to evaluate participant needs and in designing program activities to meet these needs. Parents from each school act as liaison personnel between the school and community. Aides are specially trained to assist parents with reinforcement learning activities to be used in the home.

The high enthusiasm and competency exhibited by project staff members have been generated and sustained through an in-service training program made available on a year-round basis.

Results: Reading achievement scores have shown a dramatic increase as evidenced by standardized tests. First graders jumped from 1.6 to 2.7 and second graders from 2.2 to 2.9, for example. Similar gains were recorded for other grades.

High-School Work-Study Programs

Exemplary Programs: High-School Work-Study

Program: Chase Manhattan Bank—New York Public School Work-Study Program

Location: New York, New York

Beginnings:

The Business Experience Training (BET) program was initiated by the Chase Manhattan Bank in New York City in response to the high dropout rate in area high schools. Chase's attempt at corrective action was designed to expose students to the business world by providing part-time employment for potential high-school dropouts from disadvantaged areas in the city. The program was perceived as a means of meeting company staffing needs through pre-employment training as well as "part of corporate civic responsibility to attempt to solve social problems."

Program Facts:

The purposes of the program are to provide students with part-time work in order to enhance their employability and to encourage them to complete their high-school education and compete in college.

At present, a total of one hundred male trainees are involved in the eighty-four-week program. Trainees are junior and senior class students from the inner-city, most of whom are black or Puerto Rican. They work a three-hour day (about thirteen hours a week) and receive an hourly wage of $2.10. The training offered is broad and student exposure is varied through job rotation techniques based on departmental needs. Group orientation for trainees is held at the beginning of training and is conducted periodically during the following five months.

Results:

BET has been in operation since 1964 and has trained over 150 young people. Of the nineteen original trainees, fourteen are working full-time, each of the fourteen intends to further his education with the help of Chase's Tuition Refund Plan. One of the fourteen young men was selected to participate in Chase's Accelerated Career Training Program, which trains superior high-school graduates and outstanding employees.

The company considers BET to be a relatively inexpensive program and feels that the greatest advantage of working with the schools is that of ease of recruitment. The school, on the other hand, cites as the outstanding positive feature the fact that "this selected group has been encouraged to go on—they have found they can get involved in higher-level work."

Exemplary Programs: High-School Work-Study

Program: Chrysler-Detroit Public Schools Cooperative

Location: Detroit, Michigan

Beginnings:

In addition to its involvement in "New Detroit," Chrysler Corporation approached the Detroit Board of Education and offered to undertake a program of comprehensive action aimed entirely at Northwestern High School, a predominantly black school. The Chrysler proposal was carefully considered by the Board of Education and by Northwestern school administrators who soon became convinced that it was completely sincere and in no sense paternalistic or a bid for publicity.

Thereafter, a working arrangement was established wherein project needs were submitted by the school for Chrysler's consideration, and other offers of project assistance were submitted by Chrysler for consideration by Northwestern High School. A high degree of cooperation now exists with the clear understanding that Chrysler Corporation does not dictate educational policy. Instead, its primary role is one of financial assistance and, where applicable, expert counsel and guidance.

Program Facts:

The first proposal involved assistance in the placement of Northwestern graduates. To meet the need, Chrysler renovated a wing of the school and established a placement office, the Chrysler Action Center, where testing and interviewing activities are conducted by Chrysler personnel. Thus, all graduating seniors are tested and interviewed for job placement in either Chrysler's Detroit locations or in available openings with other companies.

In June, 1968, a special summer program was instituted in which auto shop training and language arts were offered to ninety-four potential dropouts who received a $5-a-day stipend while attending. Of the ninety-four trainees, eighty-eight completed the special program and were offered part-time jobs the following school year.

A third approach to improving education is Chrysler's "Secretary for a Day" program in which students spend a day in an actual job at Chrysler under the supervision of a Chrysler employee. The Chrysler Corporation has also established a reading clinic for adults in the neighborhood and has extended the services of the data-processing center to adults during the evenings. Furthermore, the company has provided the school with a library of paperbacks by and about blacks to encourage reading interests.

Several other noteworthy examples of Chrysler-Northwestern cooperation exist. For example, those students who do not plan to attend college but who are interested in attending trade school may apply for Continuing Education Funds for as much as $500.

Creative-teaching grants of $300 are available to teachers who wish to develop educational programs. An example is the "zero hour" program—"zero hour" because class is convened prior to the "first hour" of 8:00 A.M.—which was initiated by a Northwestern teacher for the purpose of exposing honor students to special educational materials.

Additionally, the Northwestern Men's Club sponsors a summer basketball league for fourteen- and fifteen-year-old boys in the area (not just Northwestern students) to provide a positive recreational outlet for the youth.

Also, thanks to Chrysler, Northwestern is the only public high school in Detroit with its own bus. The sixty-passenger bus was requested by the school for field trips to supplement class work.

Finally, Project 75, a motivational program, is another good example of Chrysler-Northwestern cooperation. Project 75 entails grouping seventy-five Northwestern High School students with twenty-five Chrysler sponsors on the basis of a common interest and on a three-students-to-one-sponsor ratio. Each sponsor is proficient in a specific activity (e.g., bowling, sewing, ping pong, chess) so that he will be able to teach the student that particular skill. The activity allows sponsors and students to have a mutual interest in their initial contacts. The main objective of Project 75 is to develop a strong relationship between the three students and the Chrysler sponsor so that the students will feel free to talk about their problems, goals in life, the world of work, or just the philosophy of life.

Legislation to Curb Test Abuse

AMENDED IN ASSEMBLY AUGUST 17, 1970
AMENDED IN ASSEMBLY AUGUST 6, 1970
AMENDED IN SENATE JUNE 8, 1970

SENATE BILL   No. 1317

Introduced by **Senator Burgener**

April 3, 1970

REFERRED TO COMMITTEE ON EDUCATION

An act to add Sections 6902.06 and 6902.07 to the Education Code, relating to education of mentally retarded minors.

The people of the State of California do enact as follows:

1   SECTION 1.   Section 6902.06 is added to the Education Code,
2   to read:
3   6902.06.   Before any minor is admitted to a special educa-
4   tion program for mentally retarded minors established pur-
5   suant to this chapter or Article 10 (commencing with Section
6   895) of Chapter 4 of Division 3, the minor shall be given verbal

LEGISLATIVE COUNSEL'S DIGEST

SB 1317, as amended, Burgener (Ed.). Mentally retarded minors.
Adds Secs. 6902.06 and 6902.07, Ed.C.

Requires verbal or nonverbal individual intelligence testing of minors in specified primary home language prior to admission to a special education program for the mentally retarded.

Prohibits placement of minor in special education class for the mentally retarded if he scores higher than two standard deviations below the norm , *considering the standard measurement of error,* on a specified individual intelligence test.

Prohibits placement of minor in special education program for the mentally retarded if, when being tested in a language other than English, he scores higher than two standard deviations below the norm on a nonverbal intelligence test or on nonverbal portion of an individual intelligence test including both verbal and nonverbal portions.

Permits placement of minor in such program if he scores two standard deviations, or more, below the norm on specified individual intelligence tests and after examination by credentialed school psychologist.

Prohibits placement of minor in such class without parents' written consent obtained after complete explanation of special education program.

Exemplary Programs: Legislation to Curb Test Abuse

Location: California

AMENDED IN ASSEMBLY APRIL 2, 1971
AMENDED IN SENATE FEBRUARY 25, 1971

SENATE BILL   No. 33

Introduced by Senator Burgener

January 5, 1971

REFERRED TO COMMITTEE ON EDUCATION

An act to amend Section 4 of Chapter 1569 of the Statutes of 1970, to amend and renumber Section 6902.06 of the Education Code as added by Chapter 1569 of the Statutes of 1970, to amend and renumber Section 6902.07 of the Education Code, to add Sections 6902.06 and 6902.095 to the Education Code, and to repeal Section 6902.06 of the Education Code as added by Chapter 1543 of the Statutes of 1970, relating to the education of mentally retarded minors, and declaring the urgency thereof, to take effect immediately.

LEGISLATIVE COUNSEL'S DIGEST

SB 33, as amended, Burgener (Ed.). Mentally retarded minors.

Amends, amends and renumbers, adds, and repeals various secs., Ed.C., and amends Sec. 4, Ch. 1569, Stats. 1970.

Prohibits placement of minor in special education class for the mentally retarded unless the results of a complete psychological examination substantiates the retarded intellectual development indicated by the individual test scores. Generally prohibits such placement if minor scores *higher than* two standard deviations ~~or more~~ below specified norm but permits such placement in exceptional circumstances.

Prescribes procedures relating to obtaining the written consent of the parent or guardian for the admittance of a minor into a special education program for mentally retarded minors.

Deletes termination date re specified provisions relating to mentally retarded minors and repeals redundant provision.

Makes various findings and declarations.

Requires certain reports re pupils in special education classes for mentally retarded minors.

Operative October 1, 1971.

To take effect immediately, urgency statute.

Vote—⅔; Appropriation—No; Fiscal Committee—No.

Exemplary Programs: Legislation to Curb Test Abuse

Location: California

AMENDED IN ASSEMBLY MAY 10, 1972

CALIFORNIA LEGISLATURE—1972 REGULAR SESSION

ASSEMBLY BILL   No. 483

Introduced by Assemblyman Brown

February 18, 1972

REFERRED TO COMMITTEE ON EDUCATION

An act to amend Sections 12822, 12823, 12826, and 12848 of, and to add ~~Section~~ SECTIONS 12821.5 AND 12821.7 to, the Education Code, relating to school testing.

LEGISLATIVE COUNSEL'S DIGEST

AB 483, as amended, Brown (Ed.). School testing: scholastic aptitude.

Deletes authority of State Board of Education to designate scholastic aptitude test to be used in school testing program; deletes from definition of testing program, scholastic aptitude testing, and deletes average scholastic ability from factors to be included in required annual testing program report of Department of Education.

Prohibits school districts from administering to pupils in the district any group standardized test, or any other test, which measures or attempts to measure the scholastic aptitude of pupils, but provides that such prohibition shall not prevent any psychiatrist or qualified psychologist *or psychometrist* from administering such test to pupils on an individual basis for purposes of placement of pupils in special education classes *or for postsecondary scholarships or awards*.

Requires that scores from group standardized scholastic aptitude tests be purged from school records by July 1, 1978.

Vote—Majority; Appropriation—No;

Index